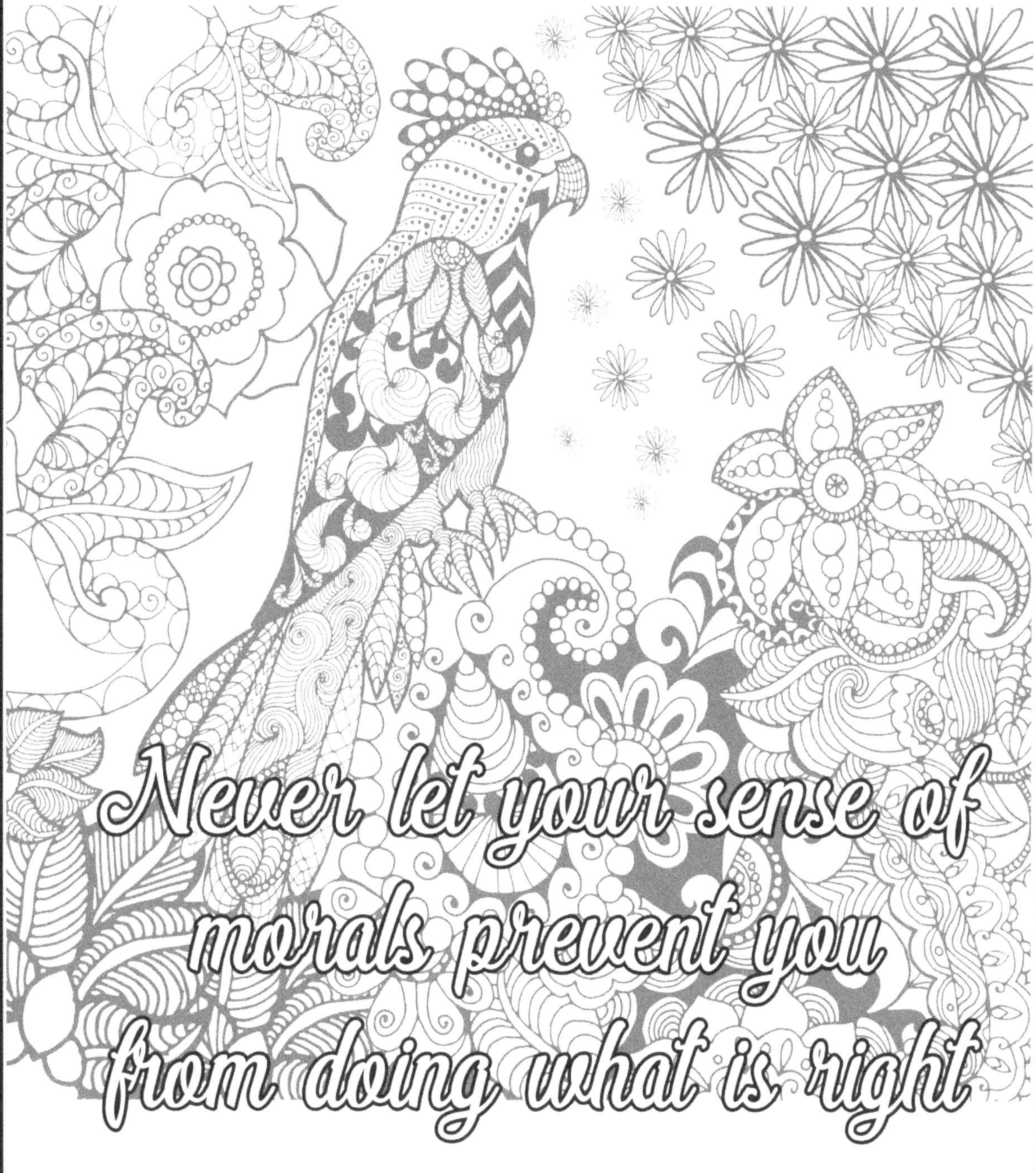
Never let your sense of
morals prevent you
from doing what is right

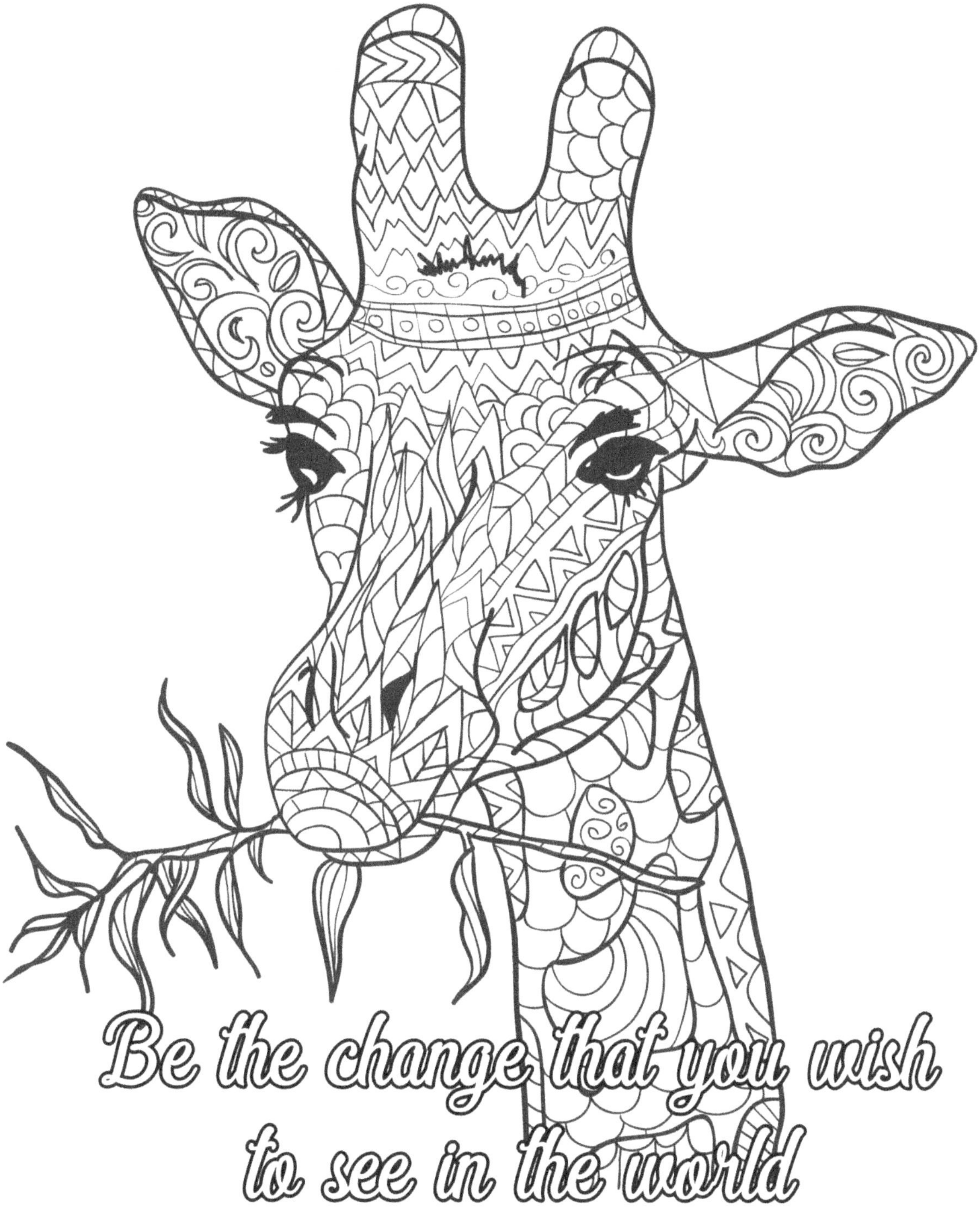
Be the change that you wish
to see in the world

May your choices reflect

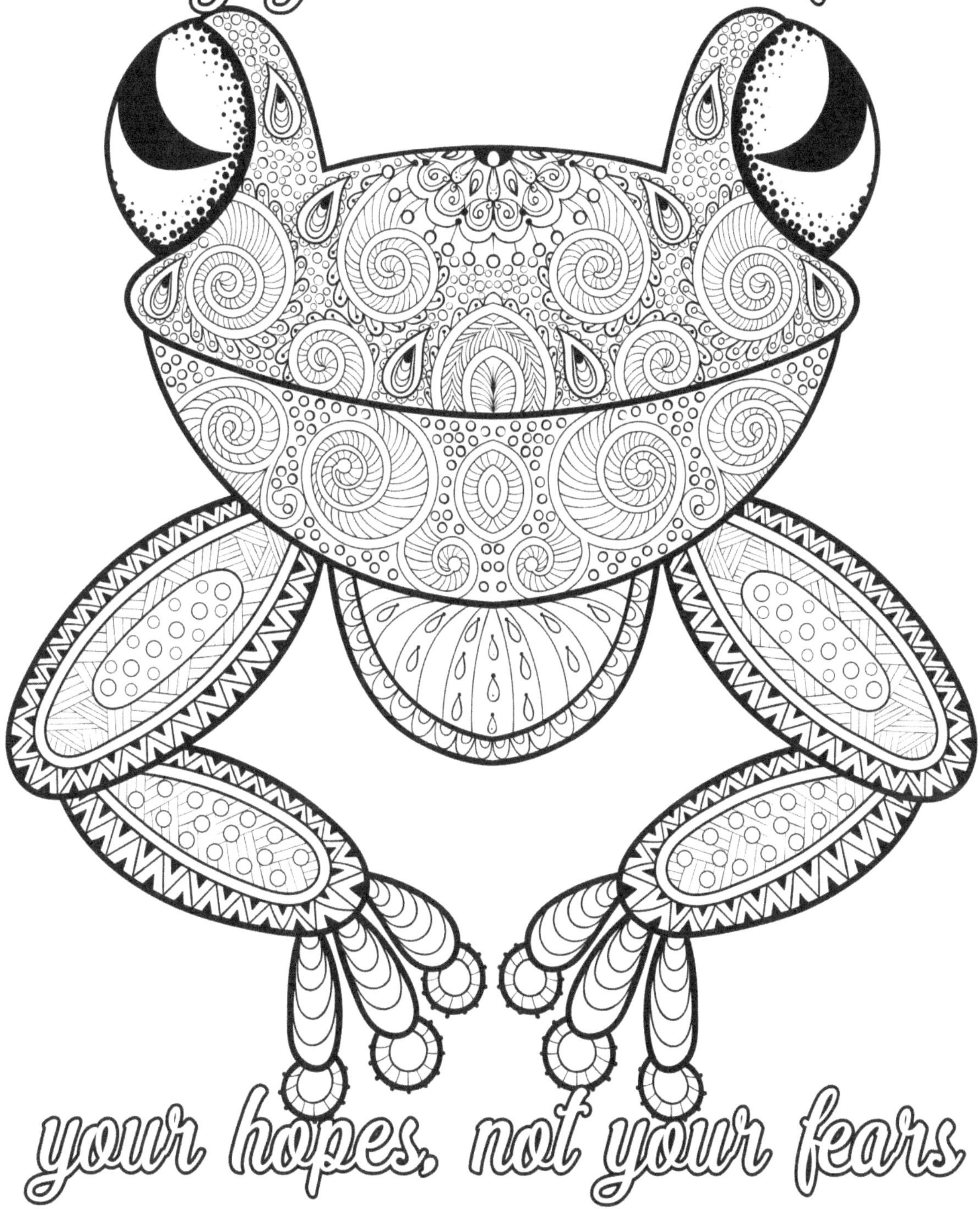

your hopes, not your fears

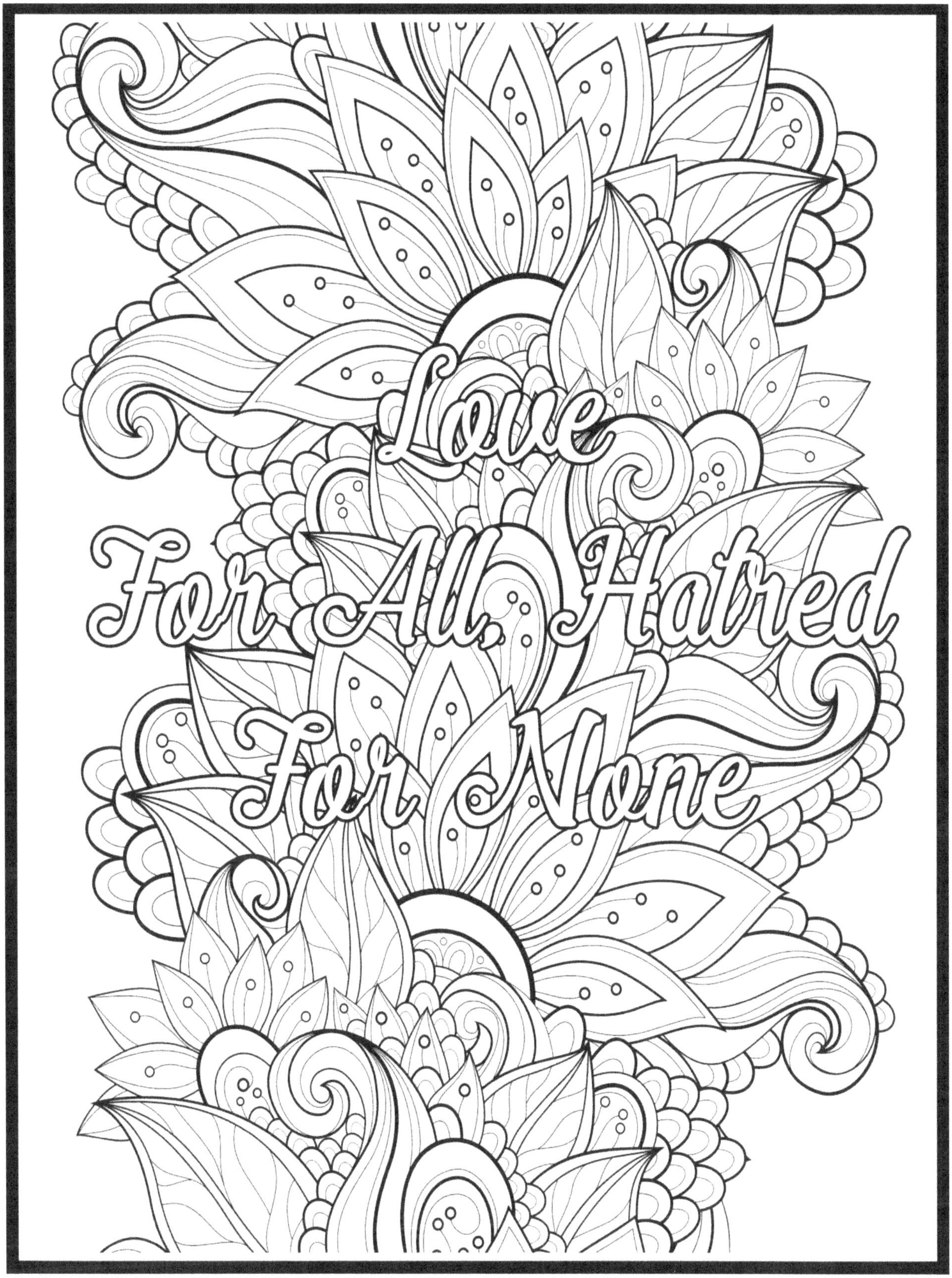
Love
For All, Hatred
For None

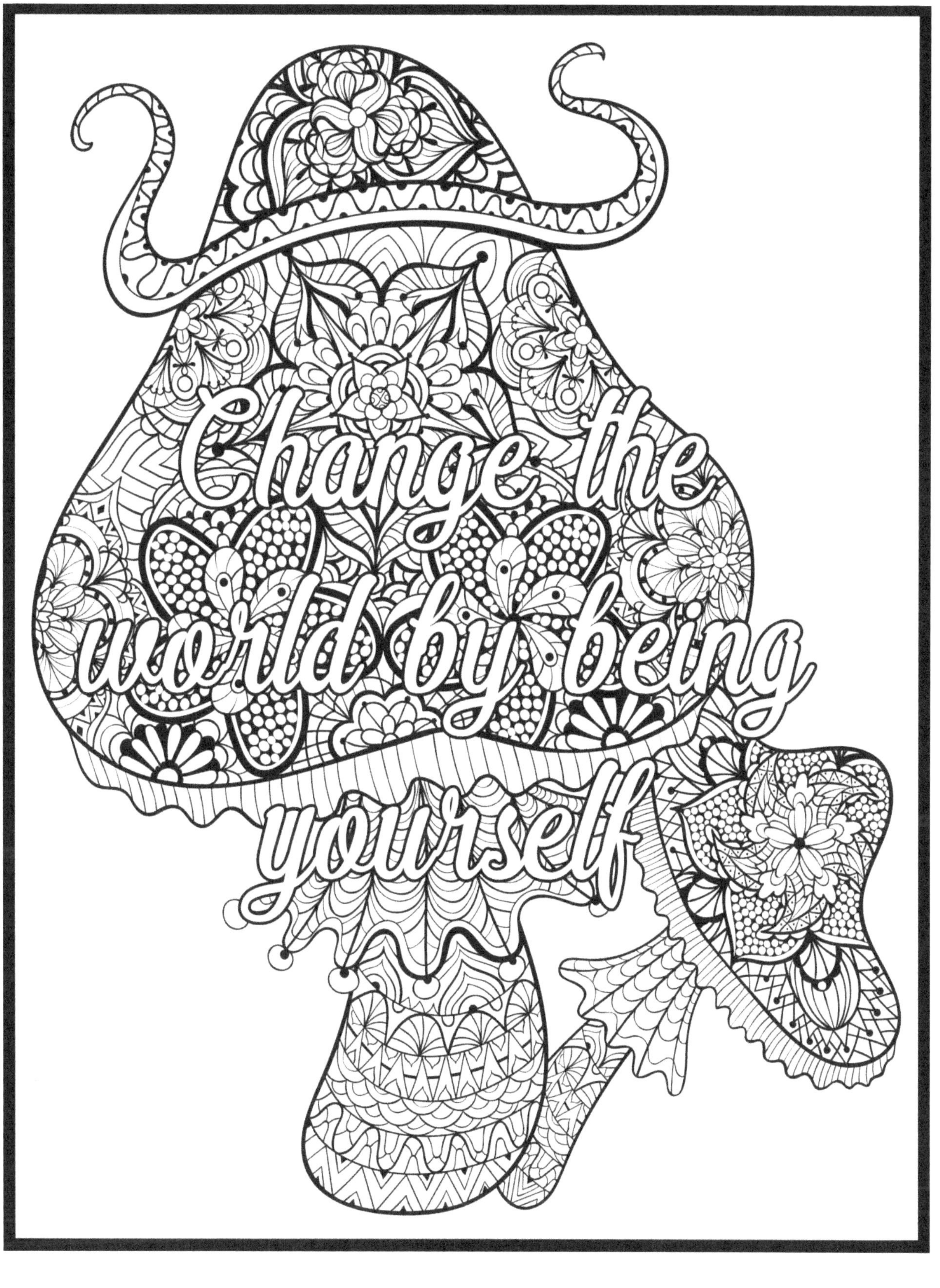
Change the
world by being
yourself

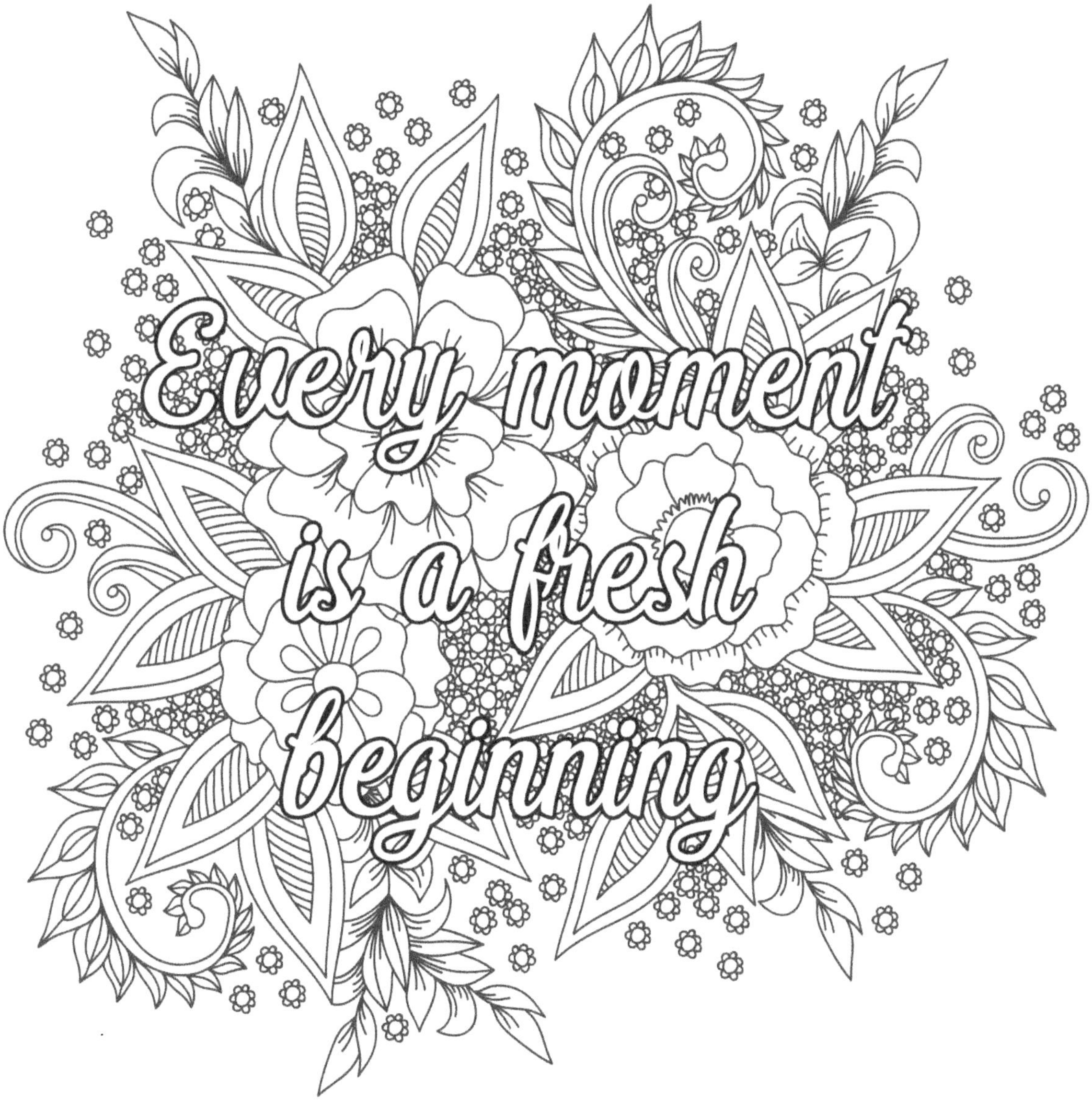
Every moment
is a fresh
beginning

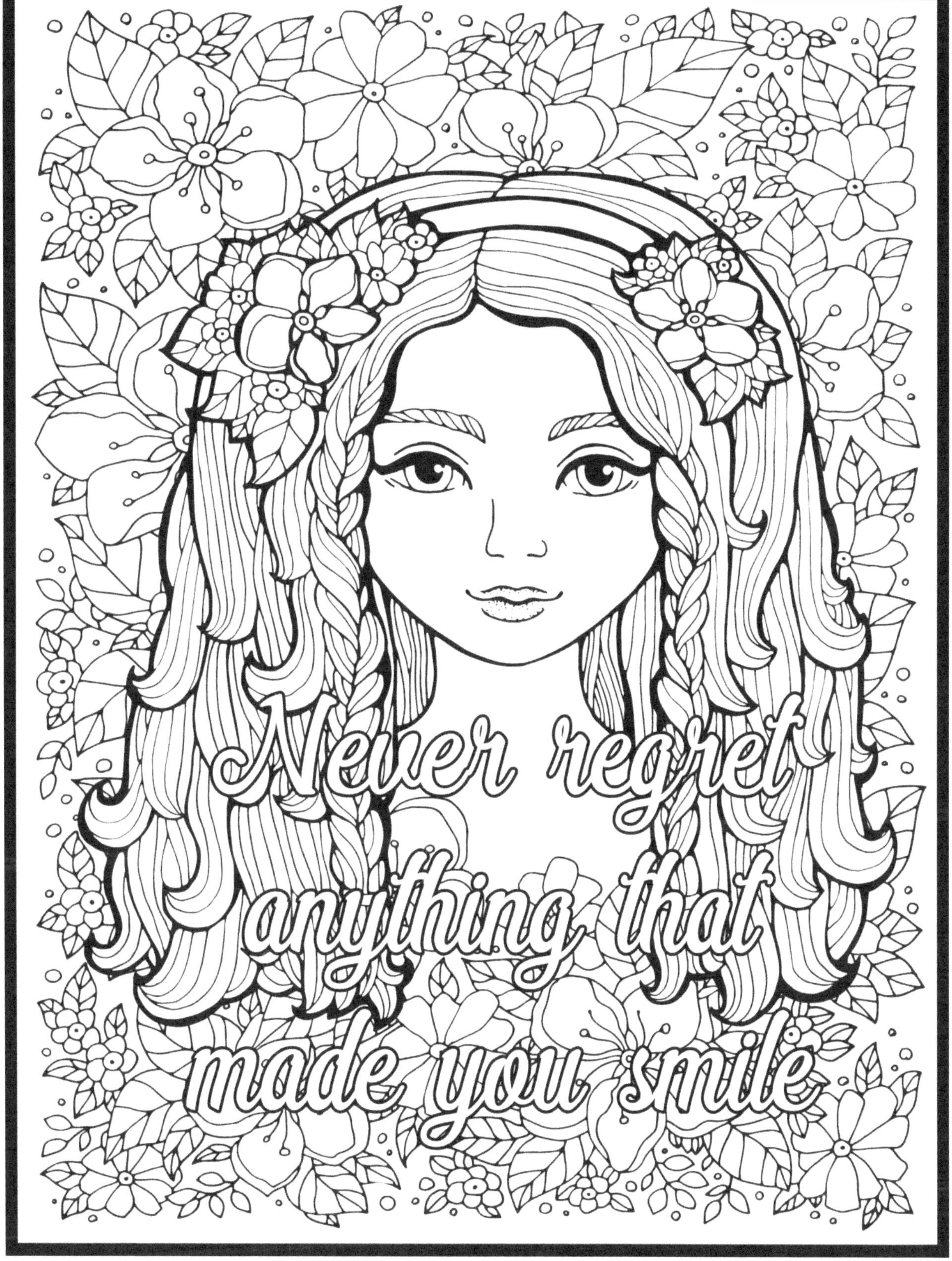
Never regret
anything that
made you smile

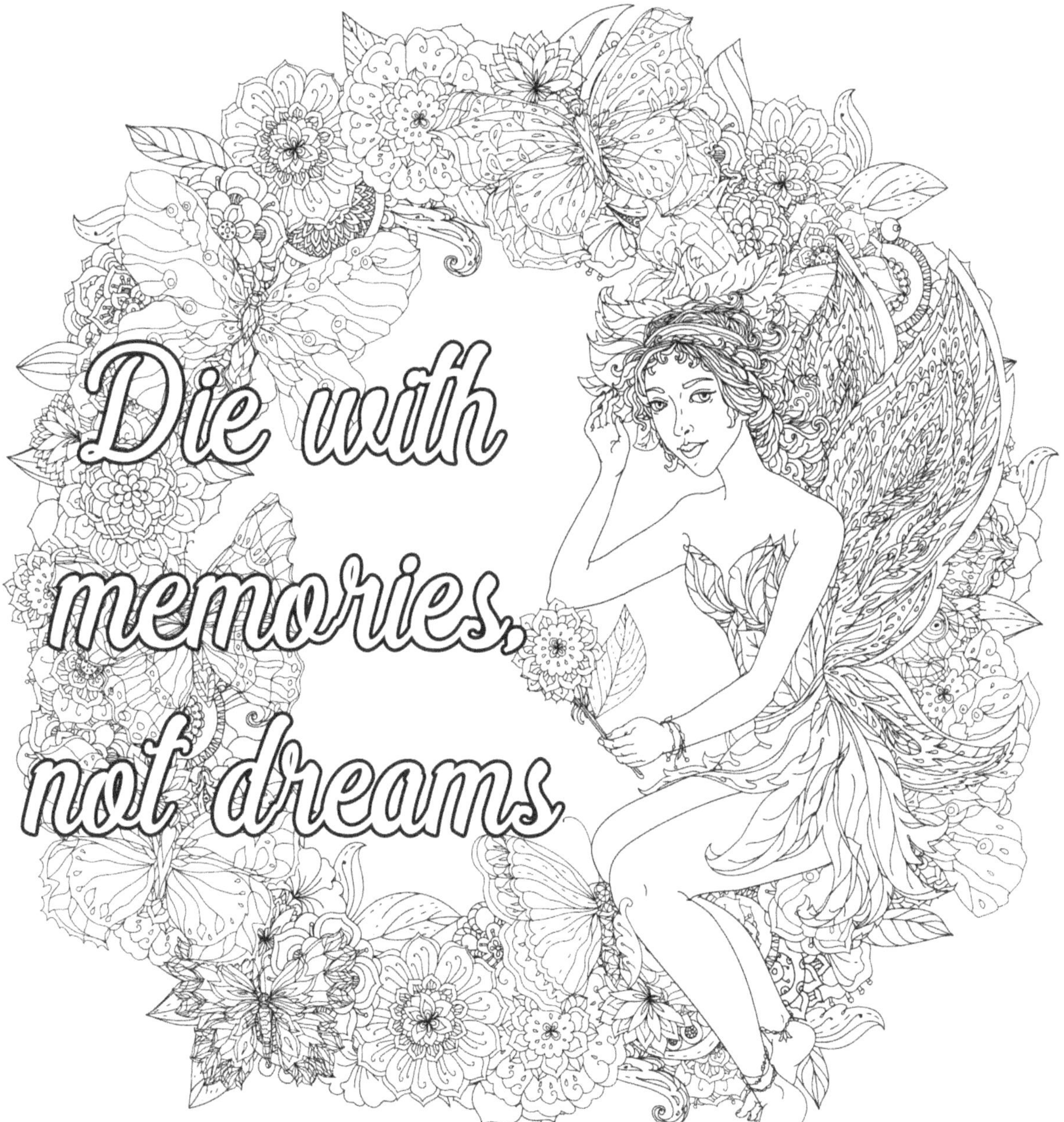
Die with
memories,
not dreams

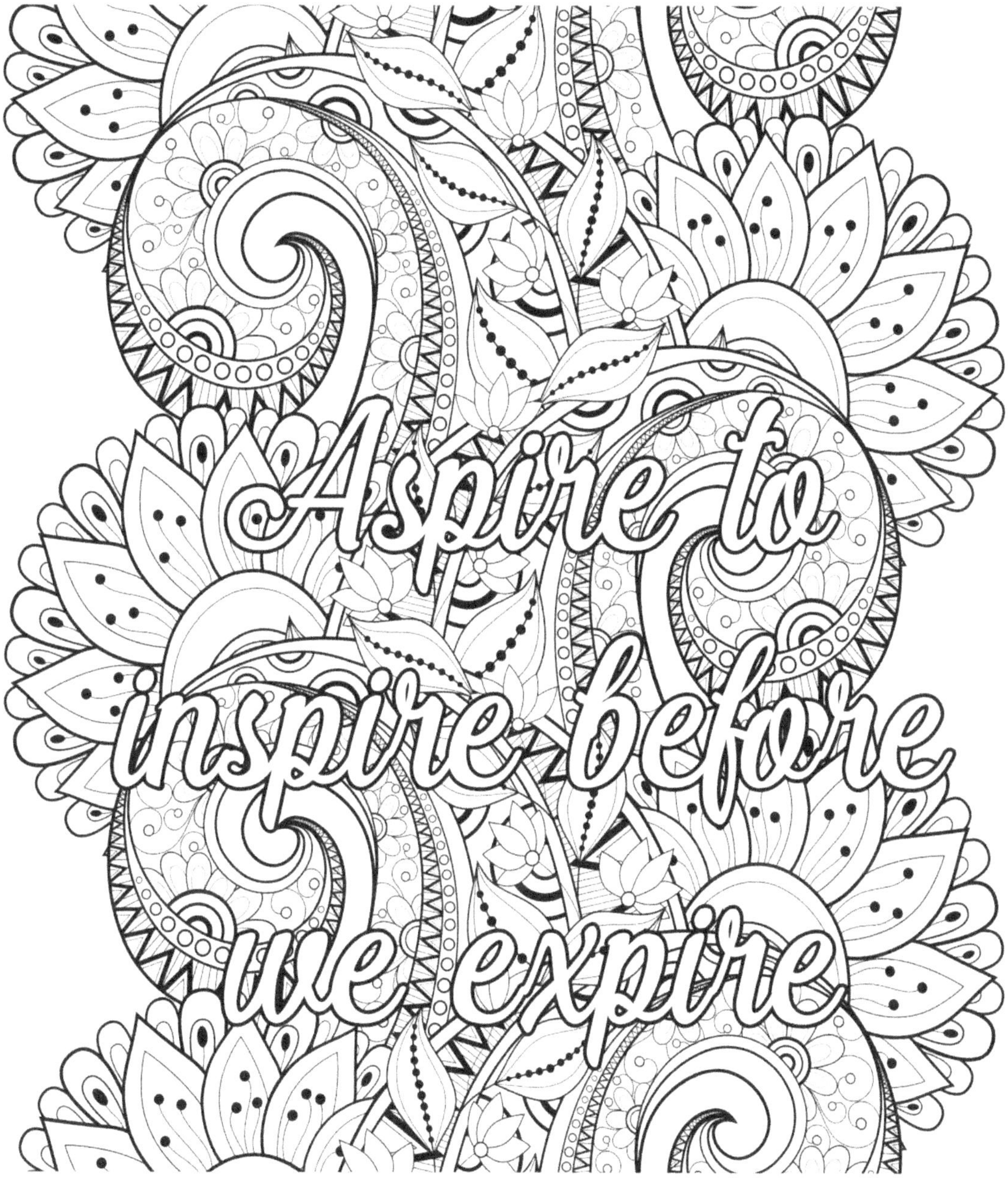
Aspire to
inspire before
we expire

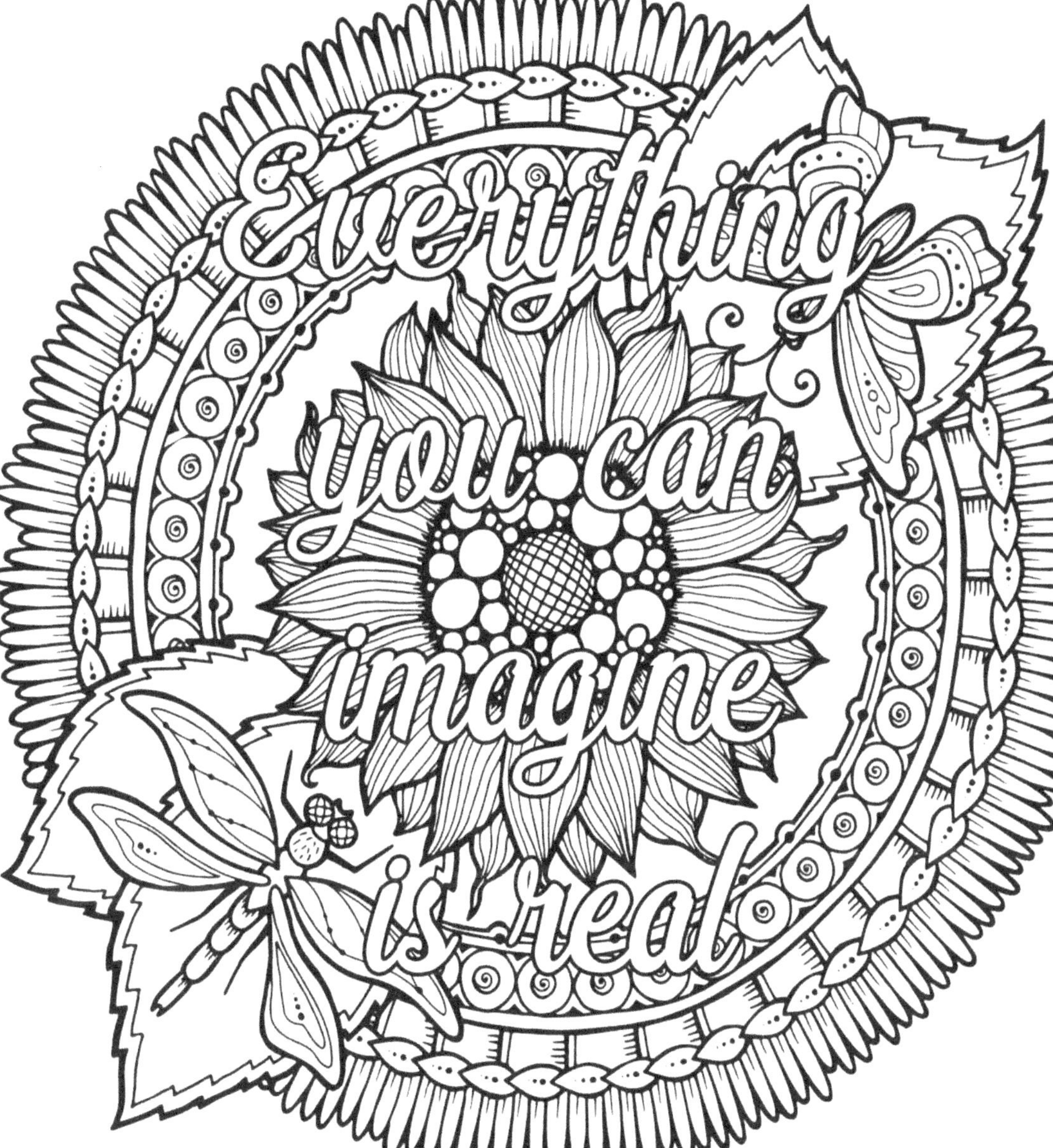
Everything
you can
imagine
is real

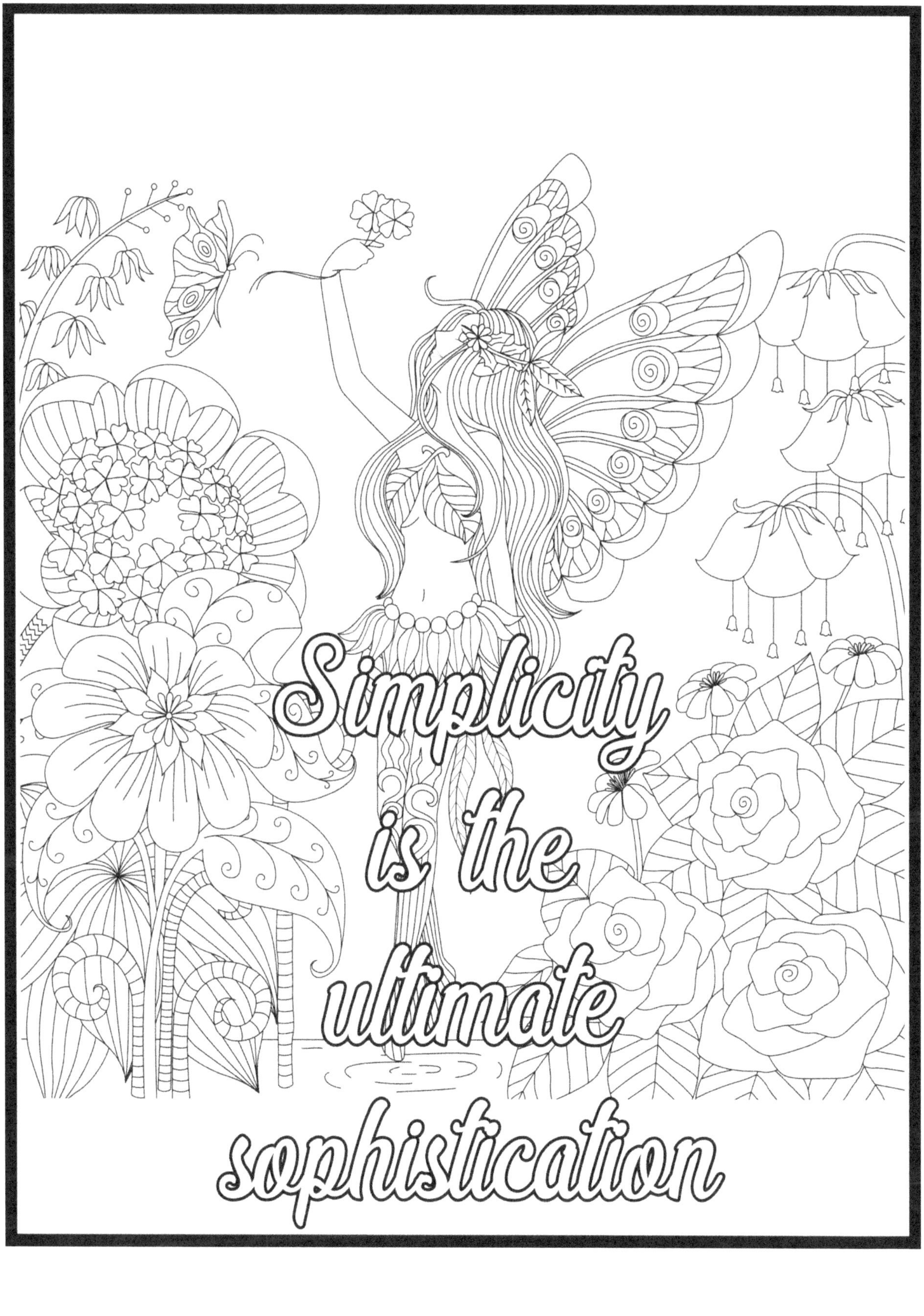
Simplicity
is the
ultimate
sophistication

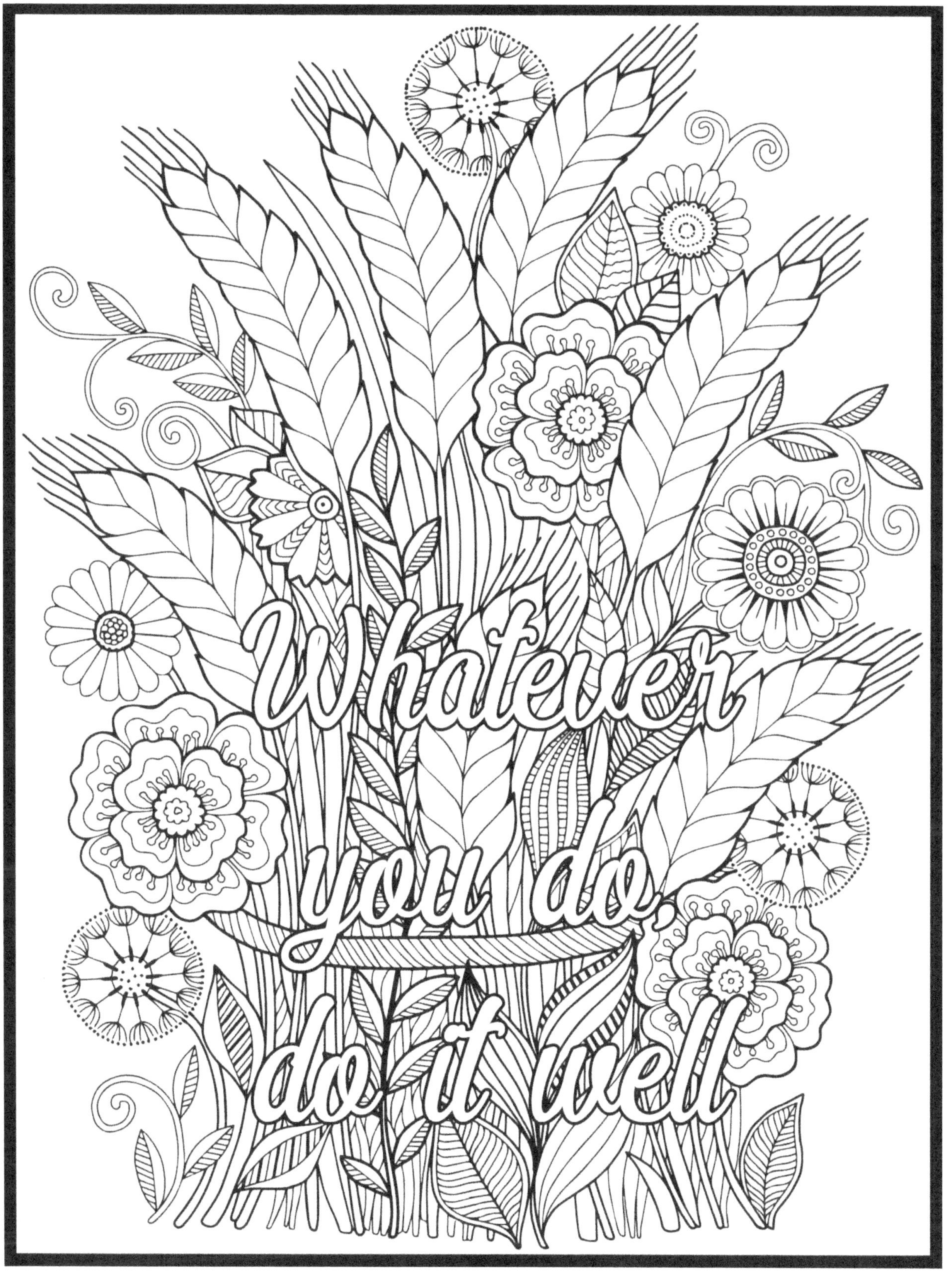
Whatever
you do,
do it well

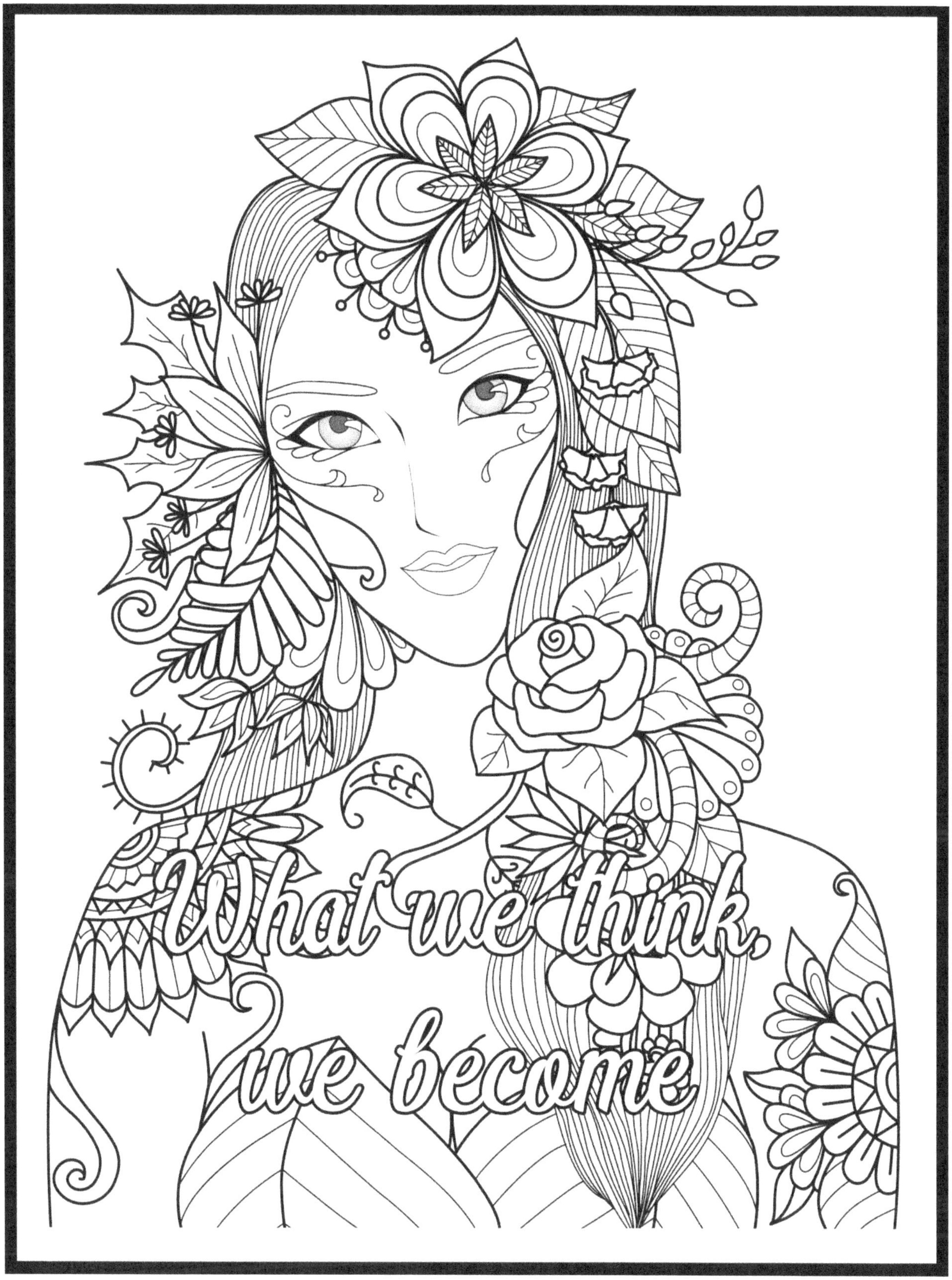
What we think,
we become

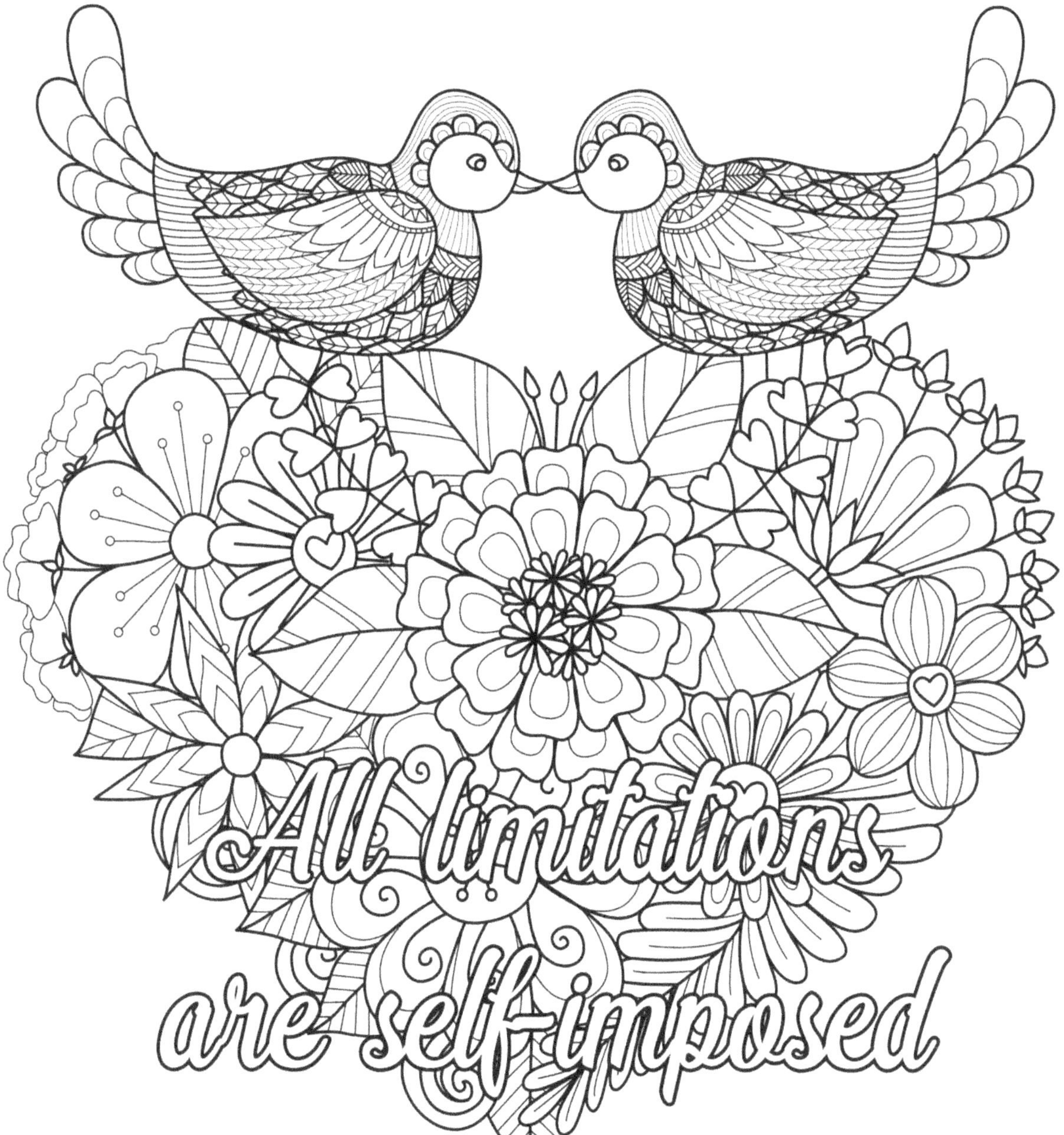
All limitations
are self-imposed

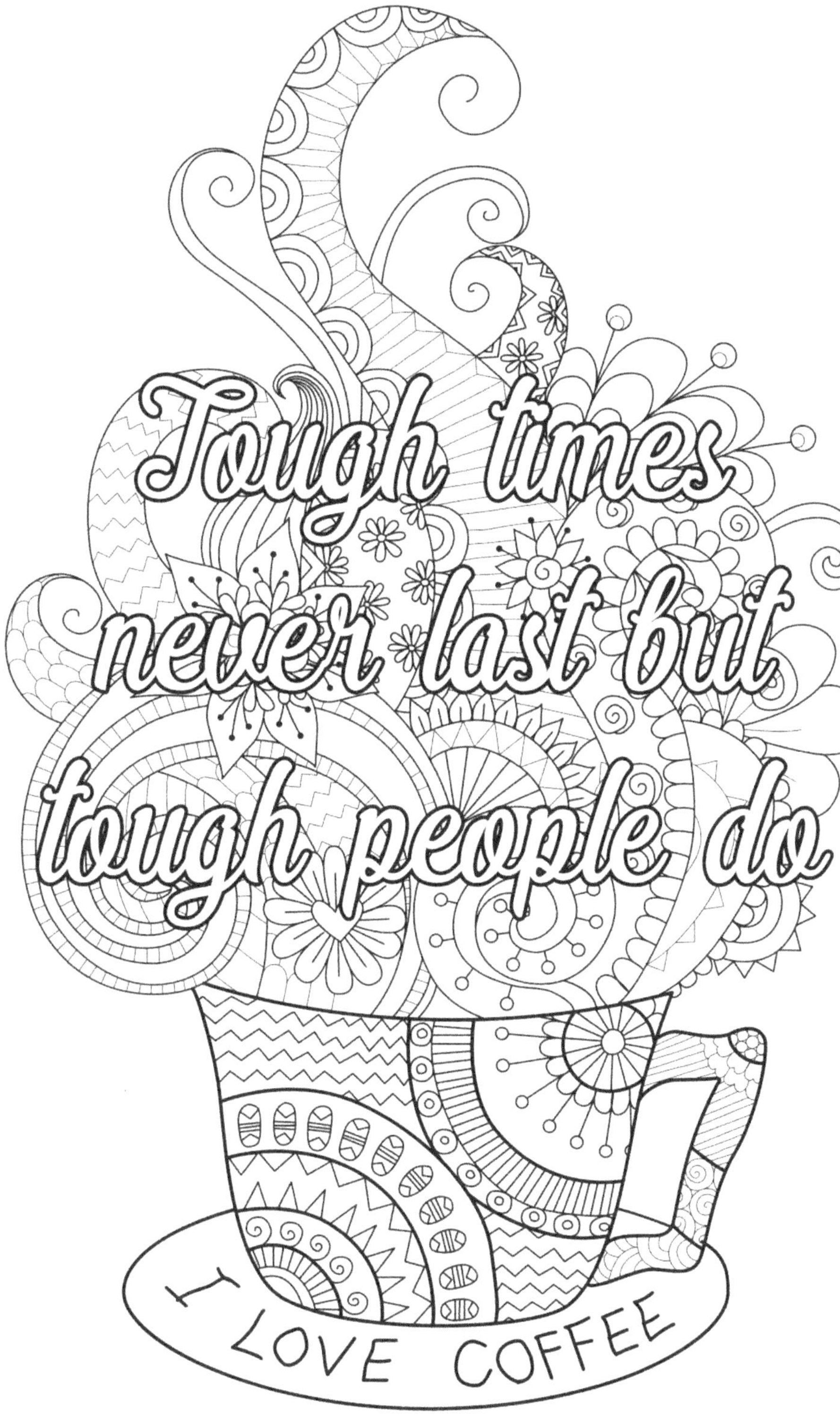
Tough times never last but tough people do
I LOVE COFFEE

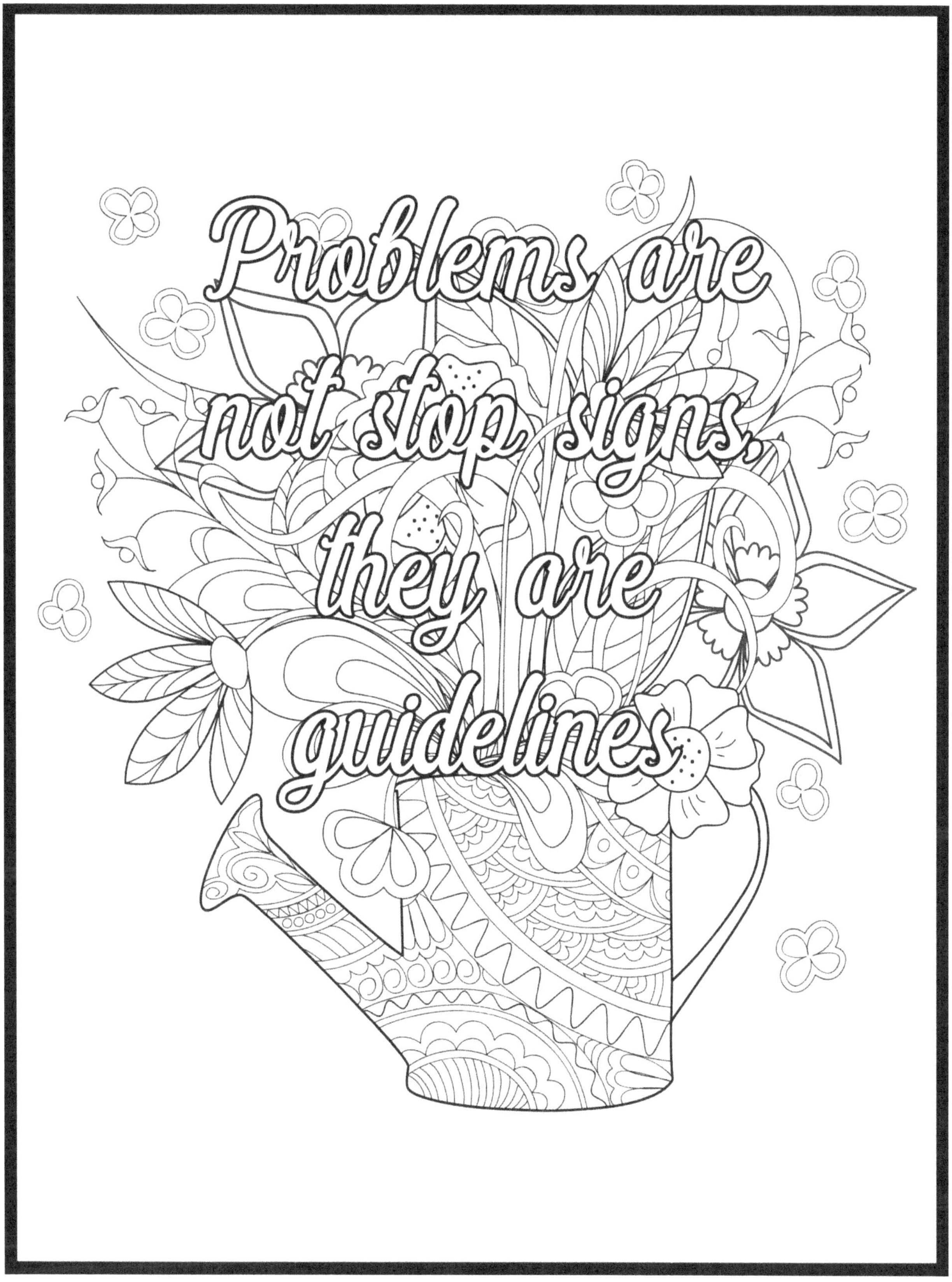
Problems are
not stop signs,
they are
guidelines.

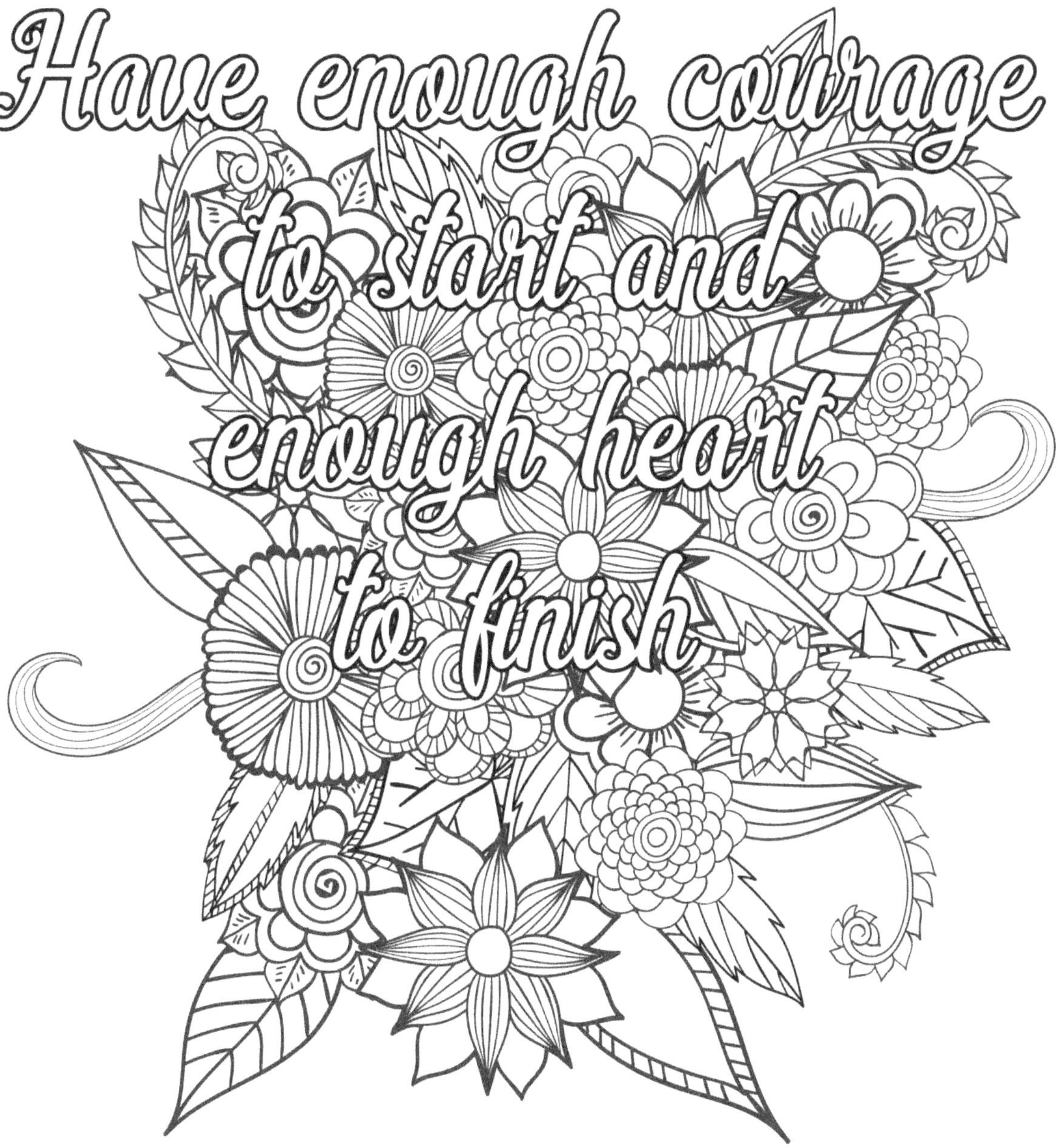
Have enough courage
to start and
enough heart
to finish

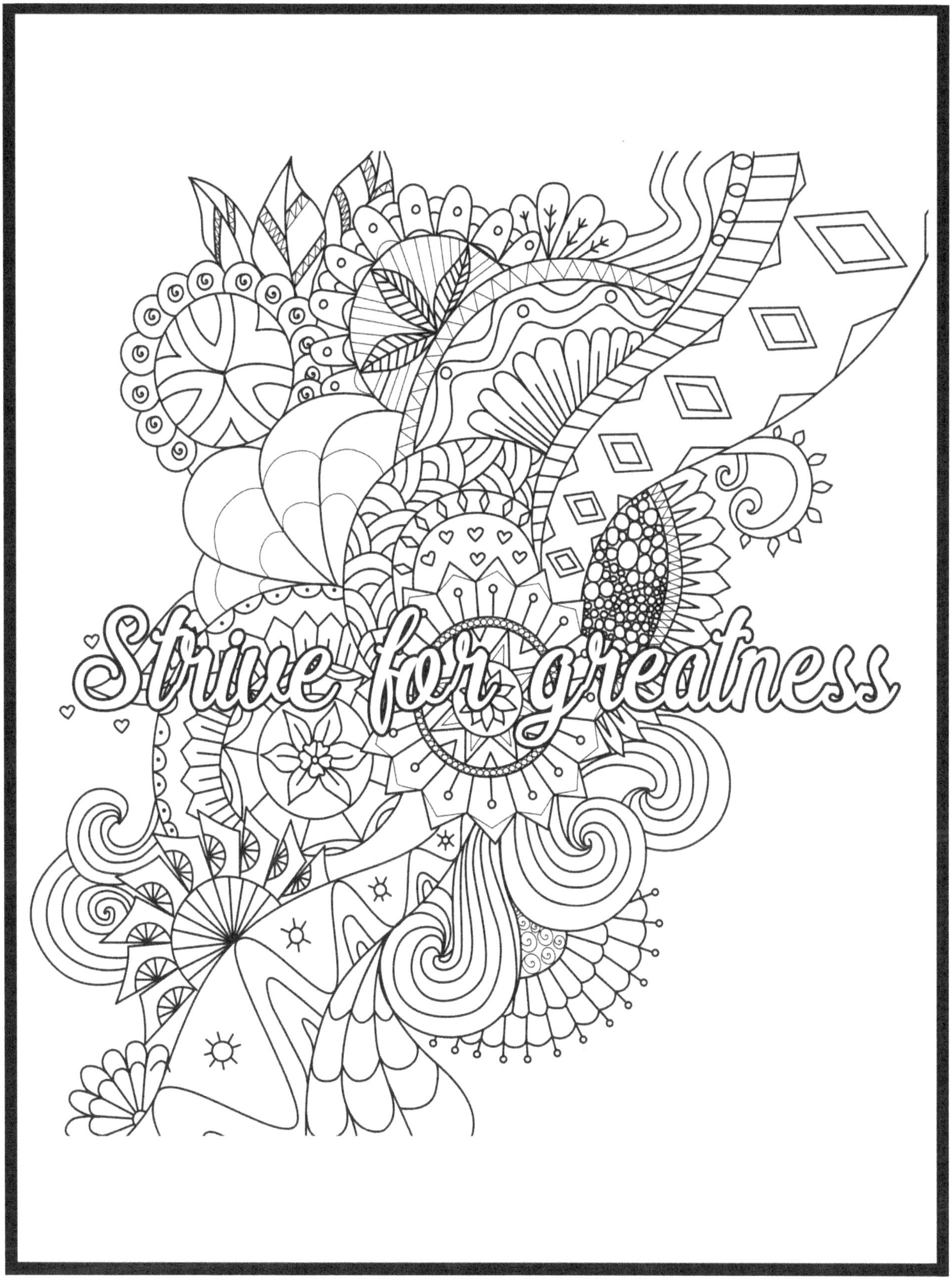
Strive for greatness

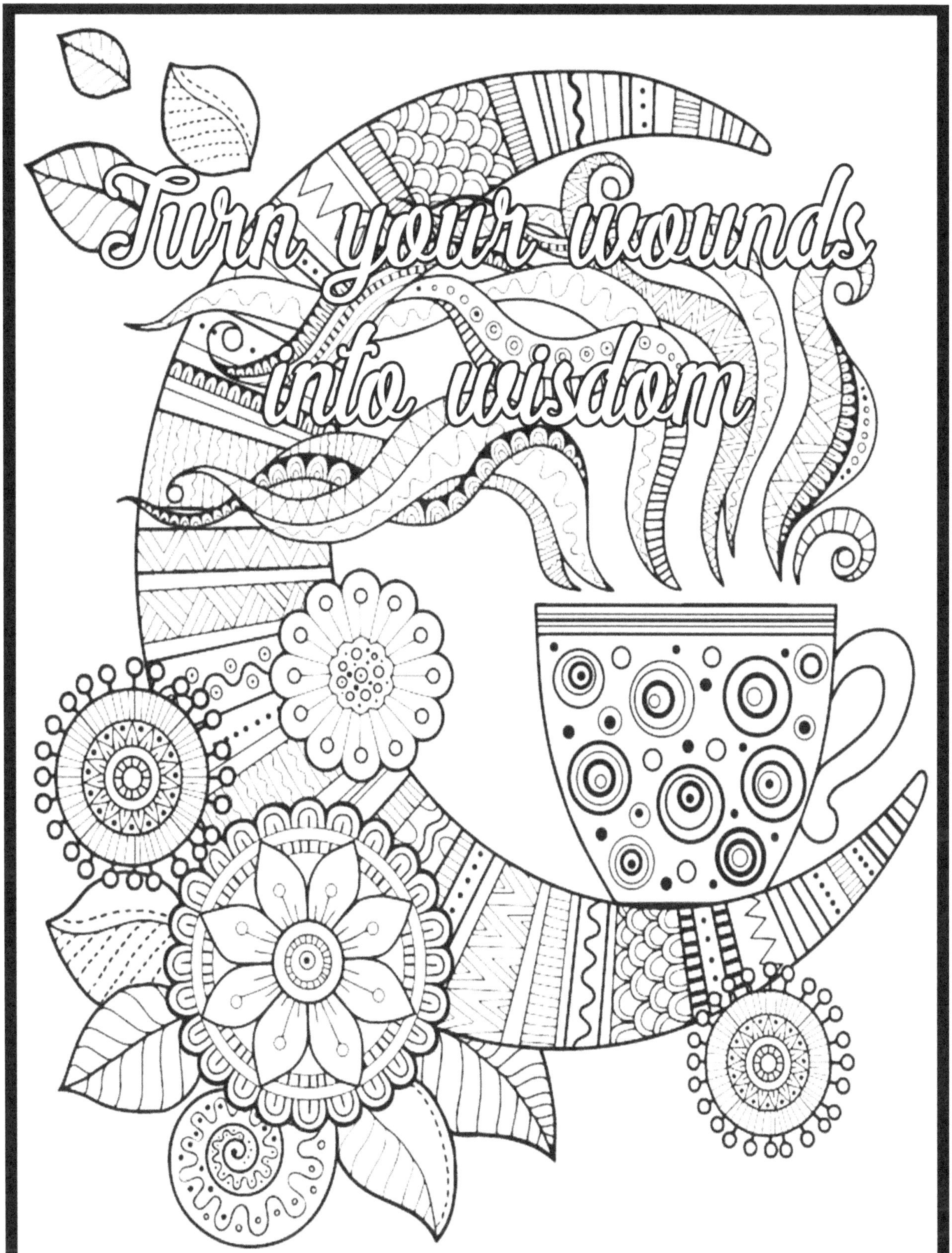
Turn your wounds
into wisdom

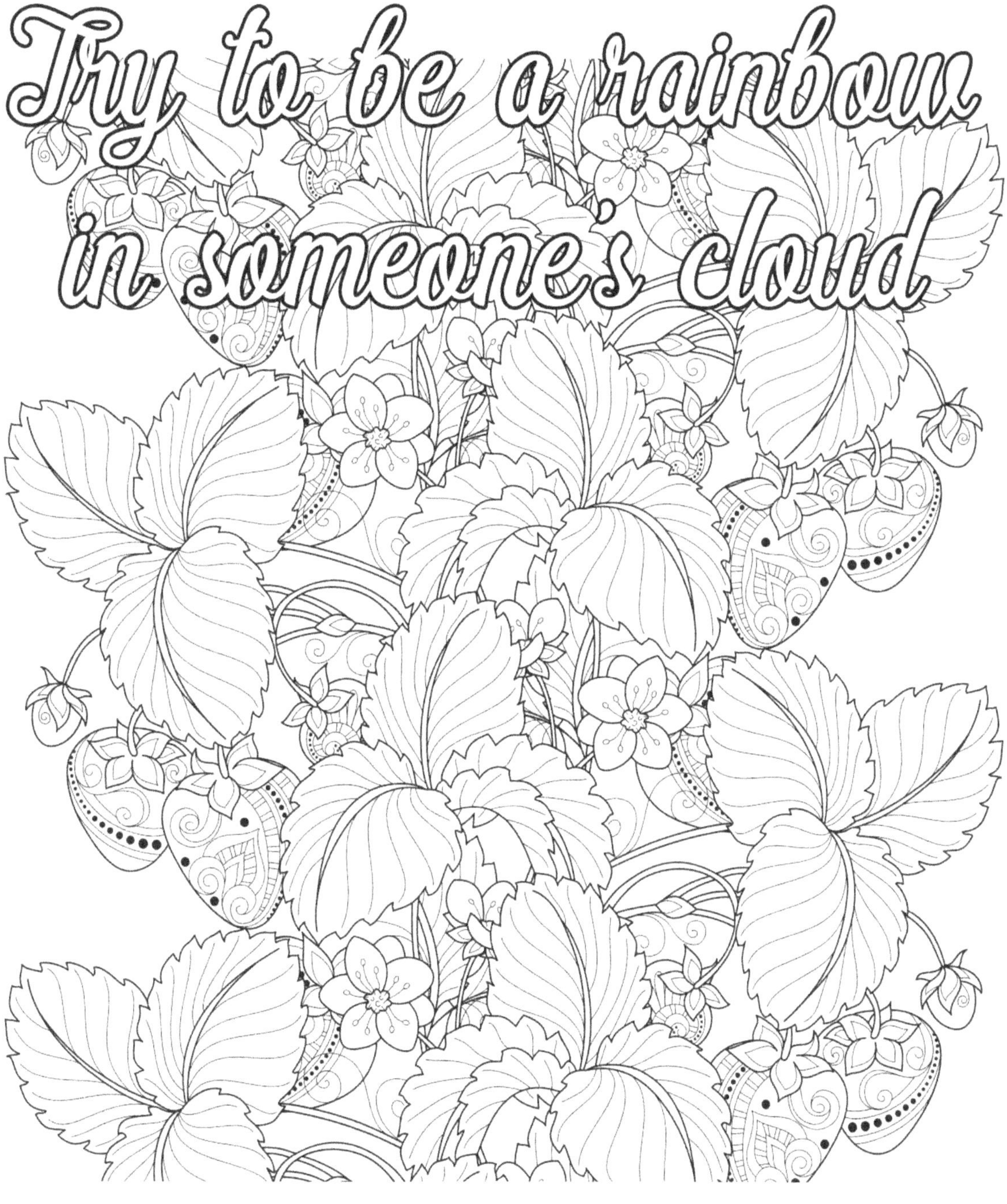
Try to be a rainbow
in someone's cloud

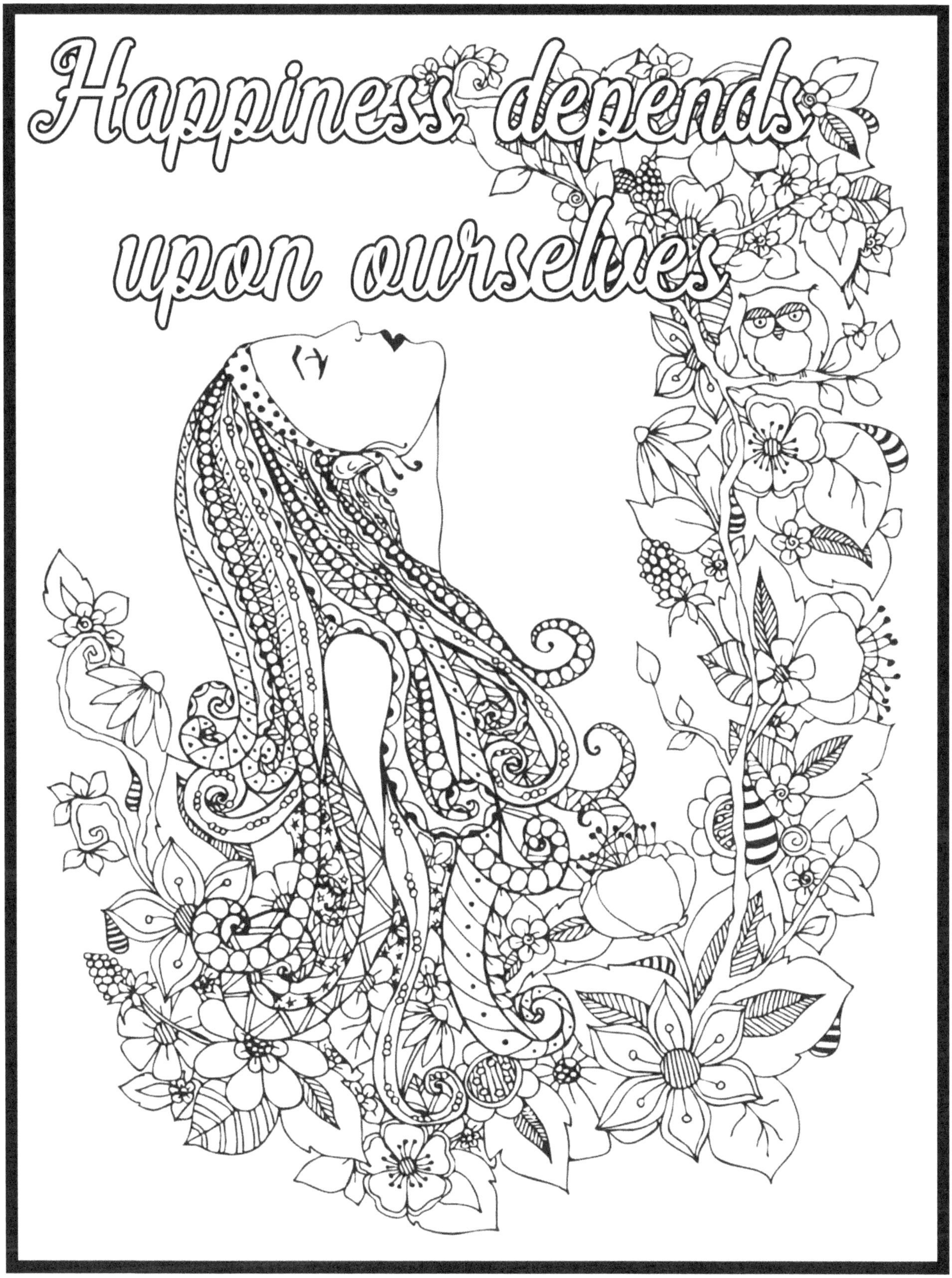
Happiness depends
upon ourselves

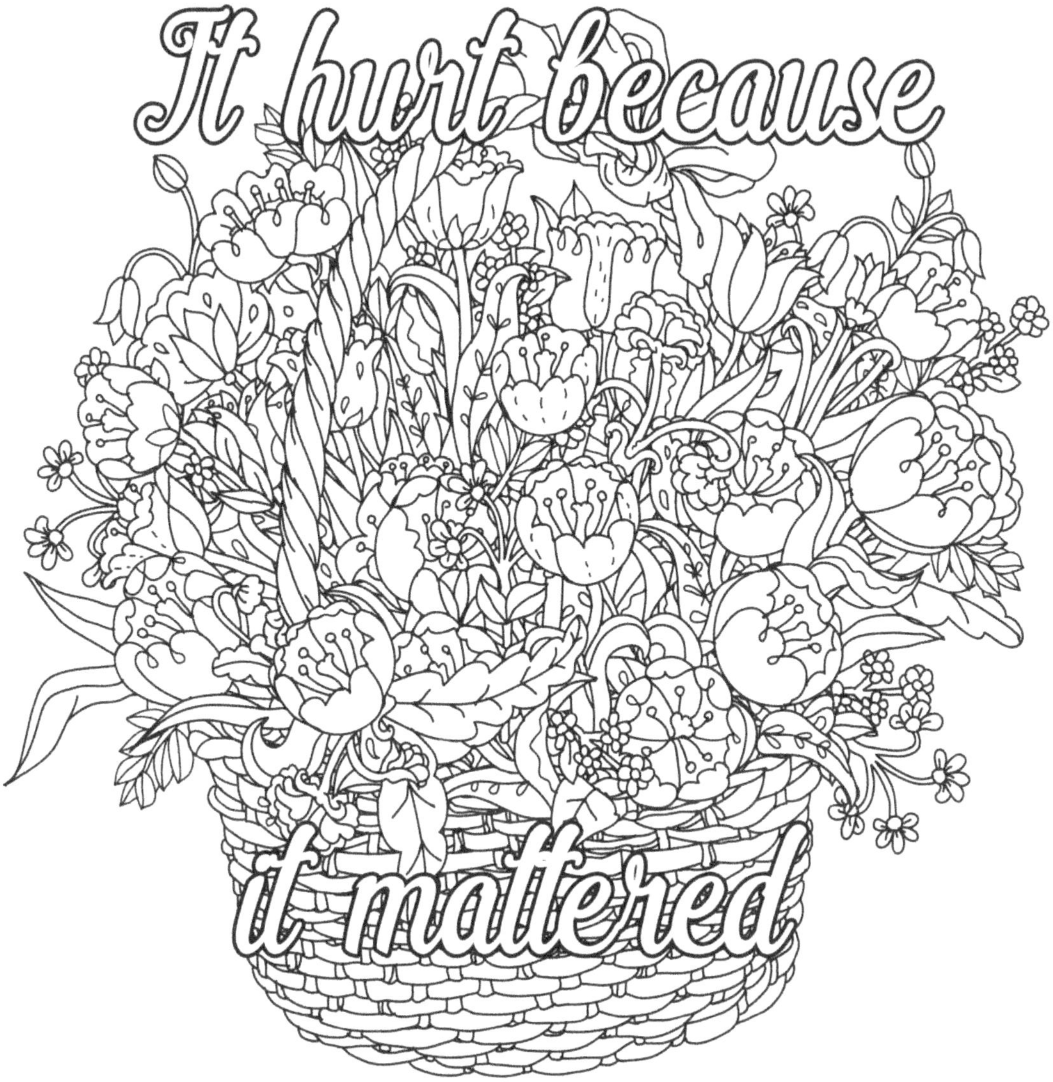
It hurt because
it mattered

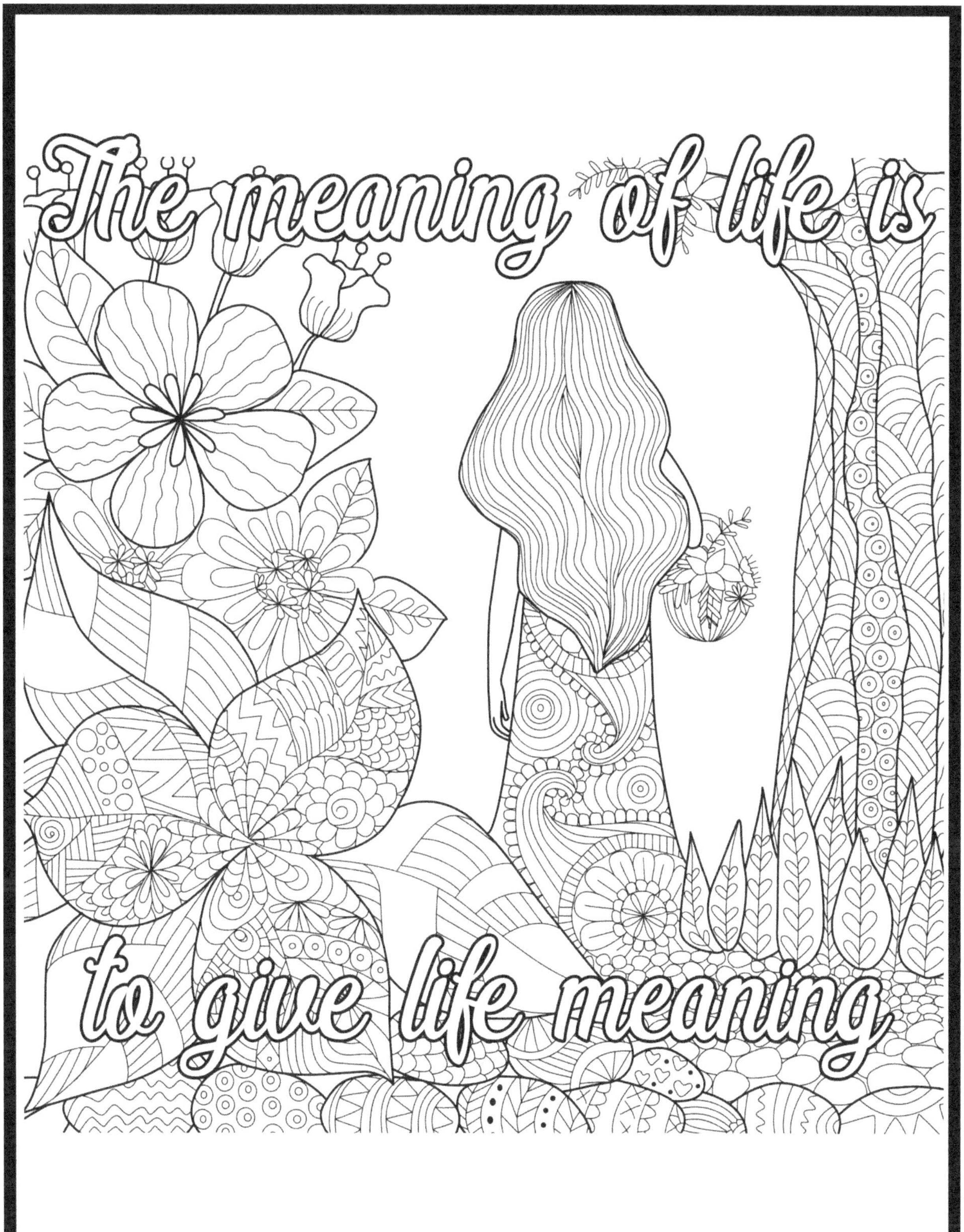
The meaning of life is
to give life meaning

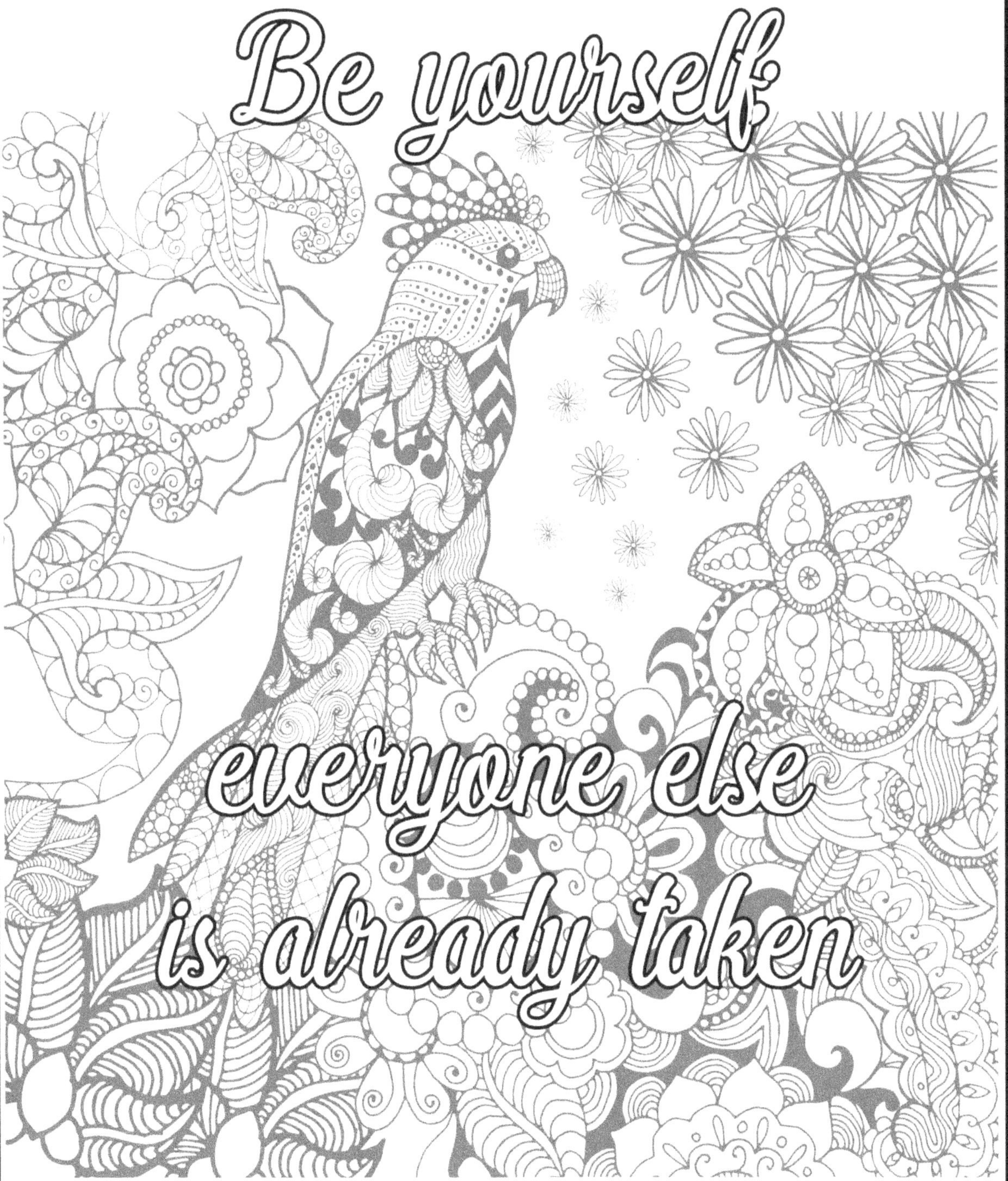
Be yourself;
everyone else
is already taken

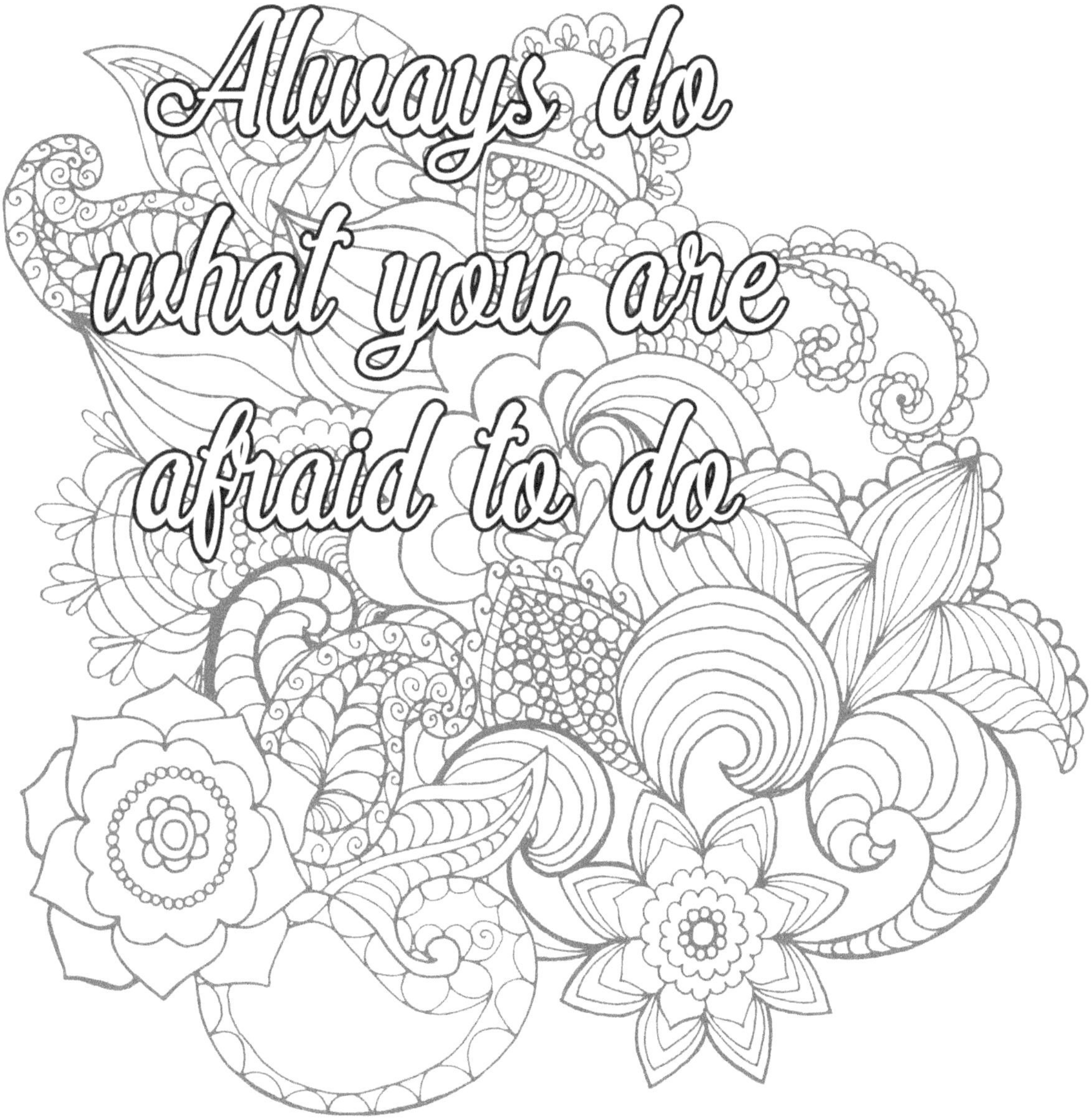
Always do
what you are
afraid to do

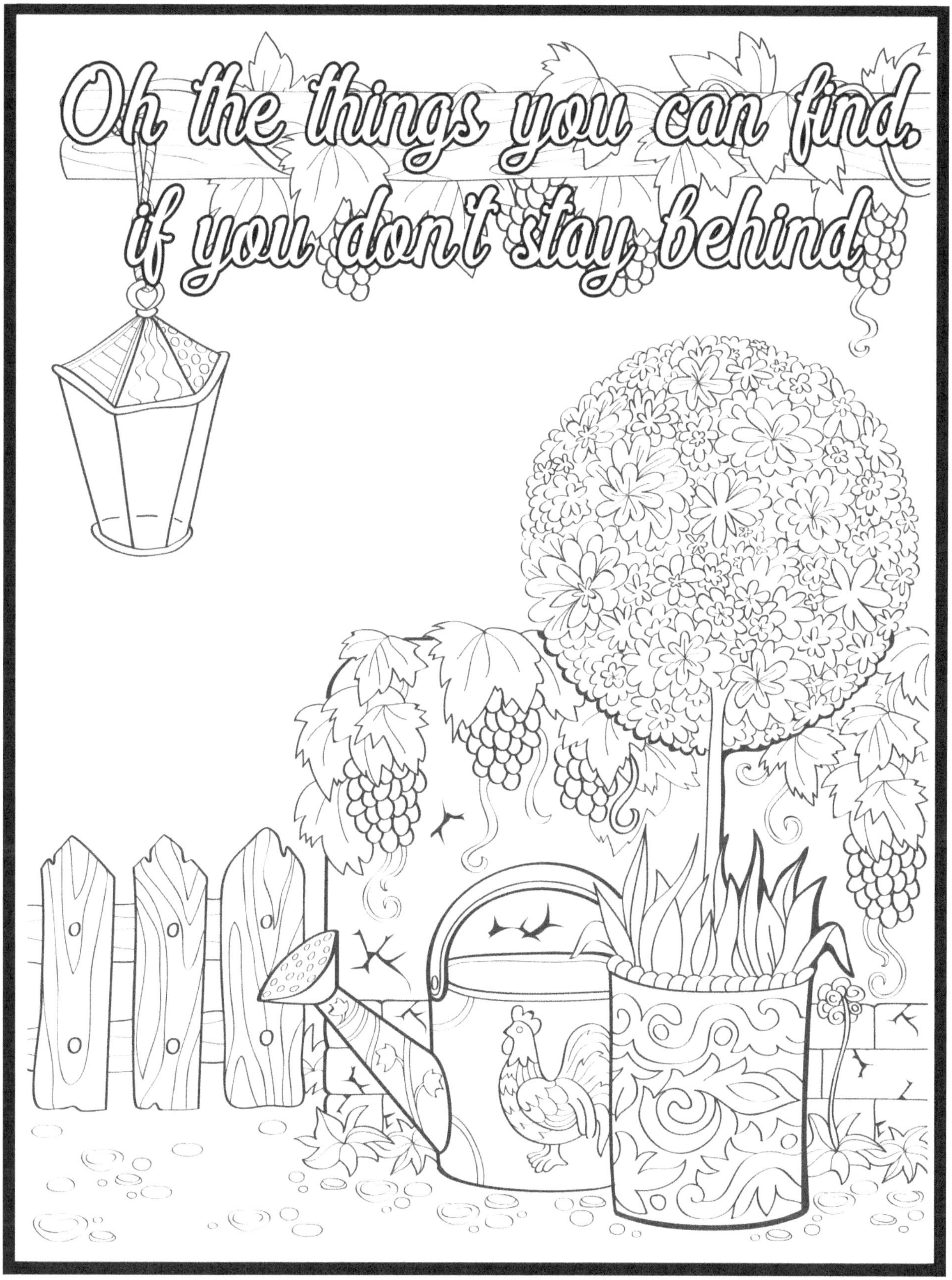
Oh the things you can find,
if you don't stay behind

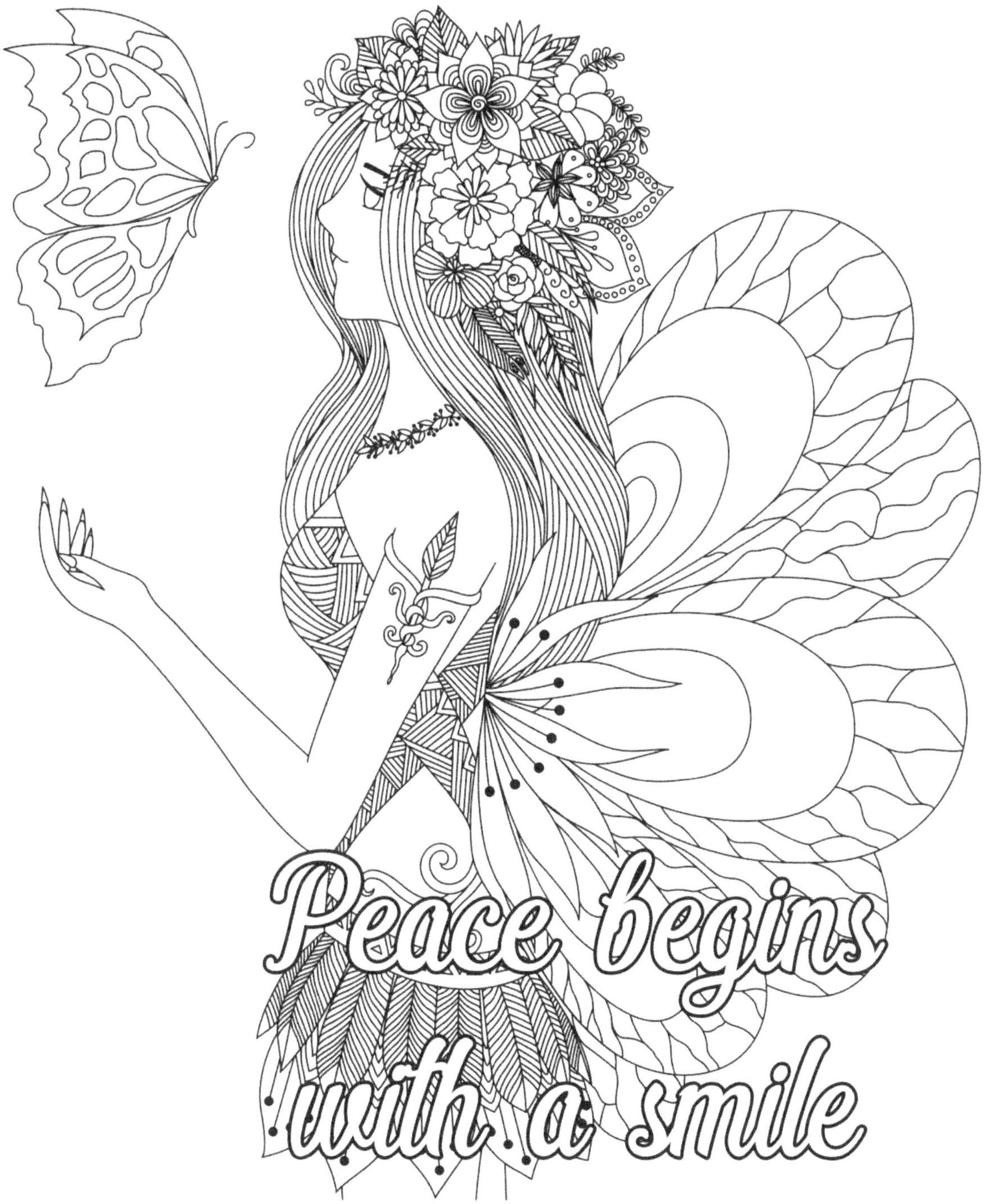
Peace begins
with a smile

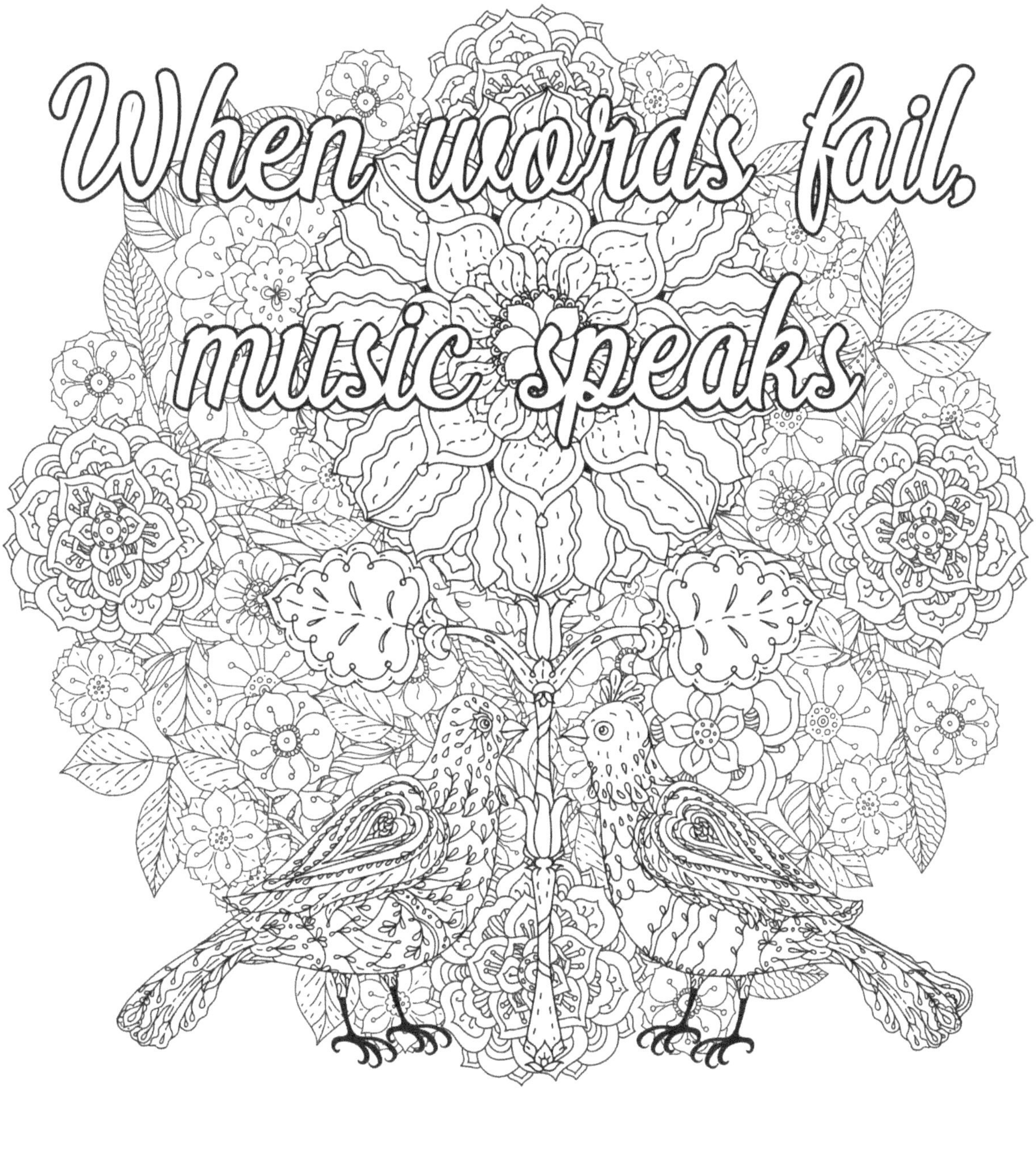
When words fail,
music speaks

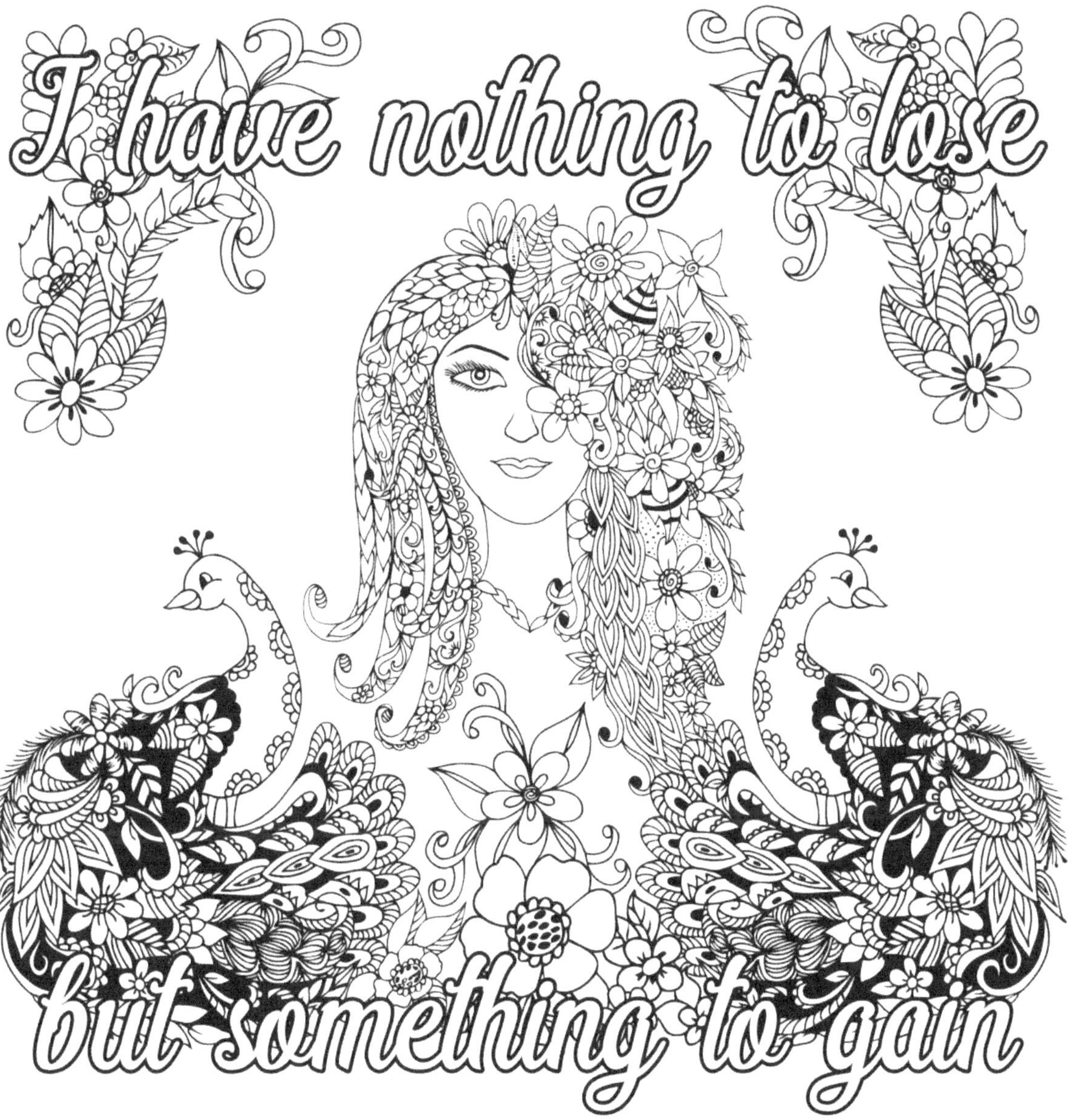
I have nothing to lose
but something to gain

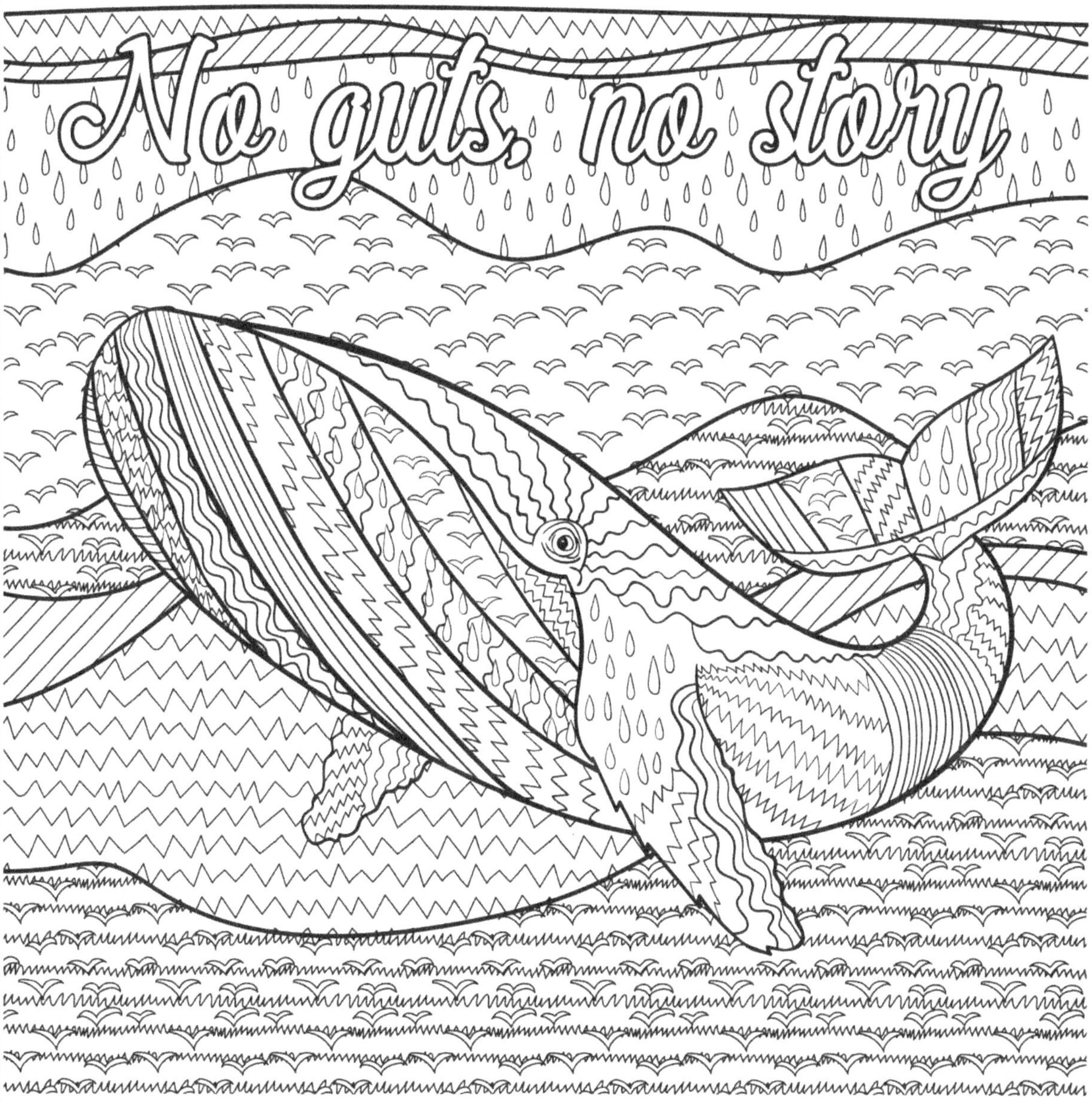
No guts, no story

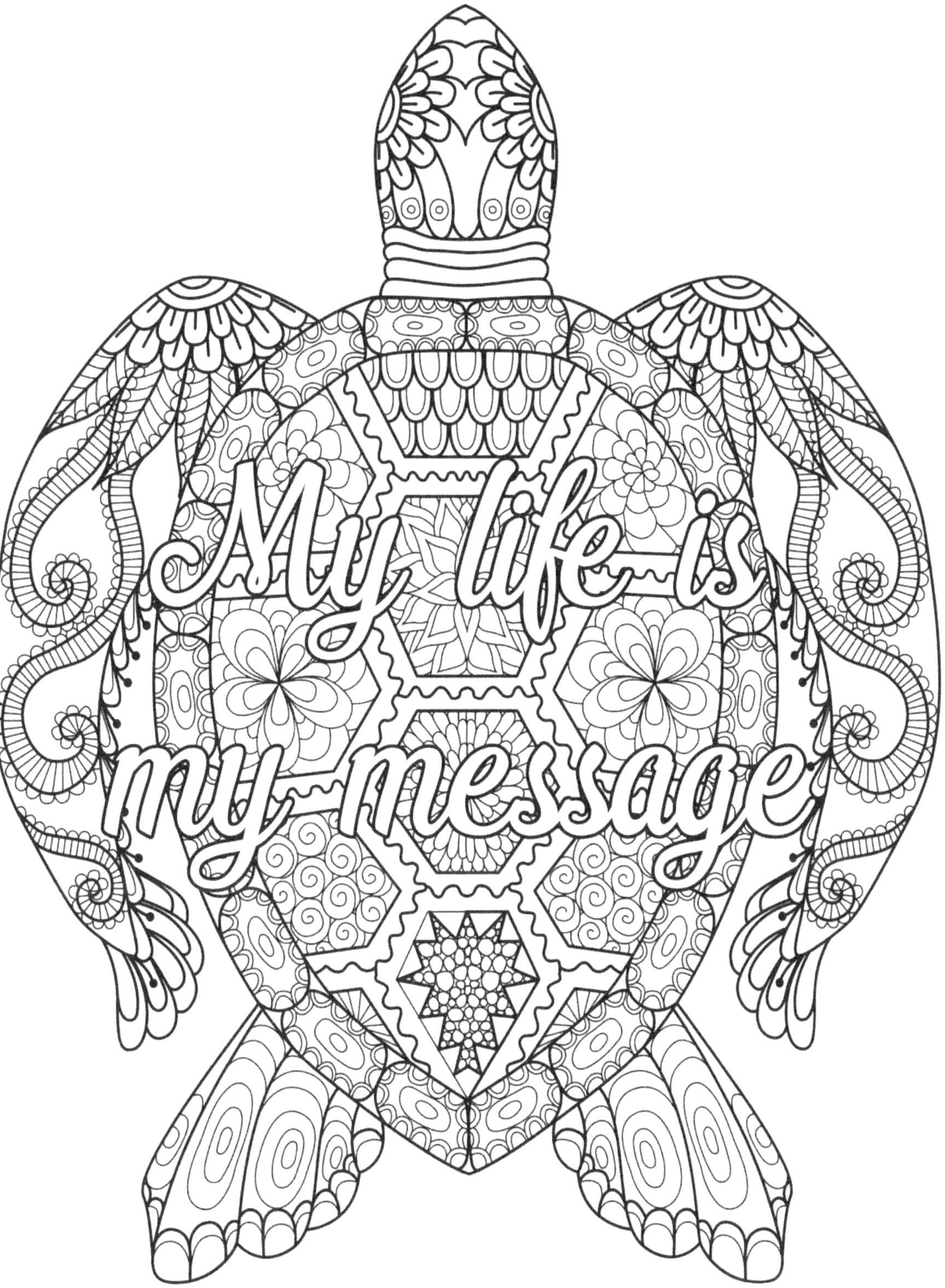
My life is
my message

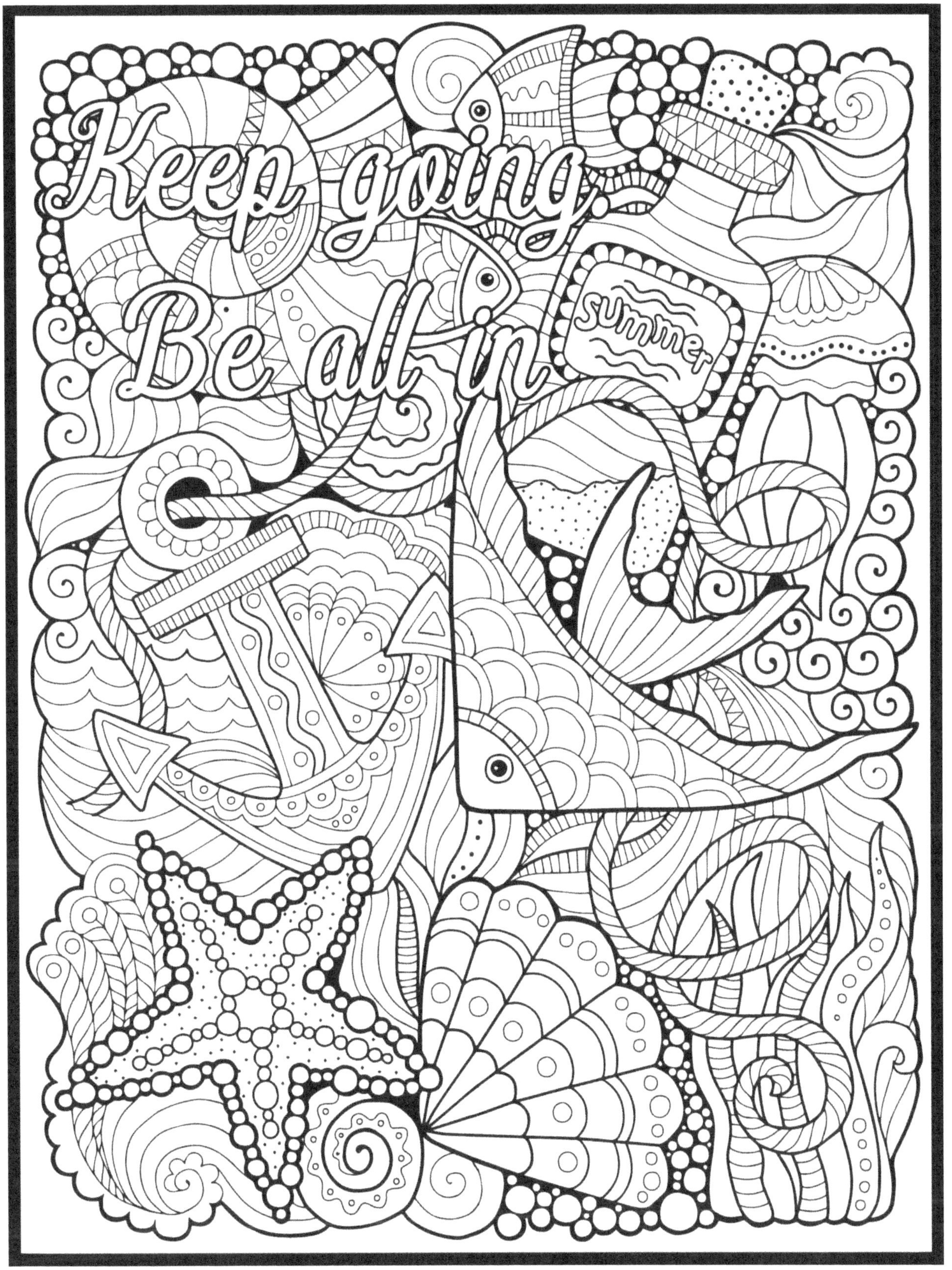
Keep going.
Be all in
SUMMER

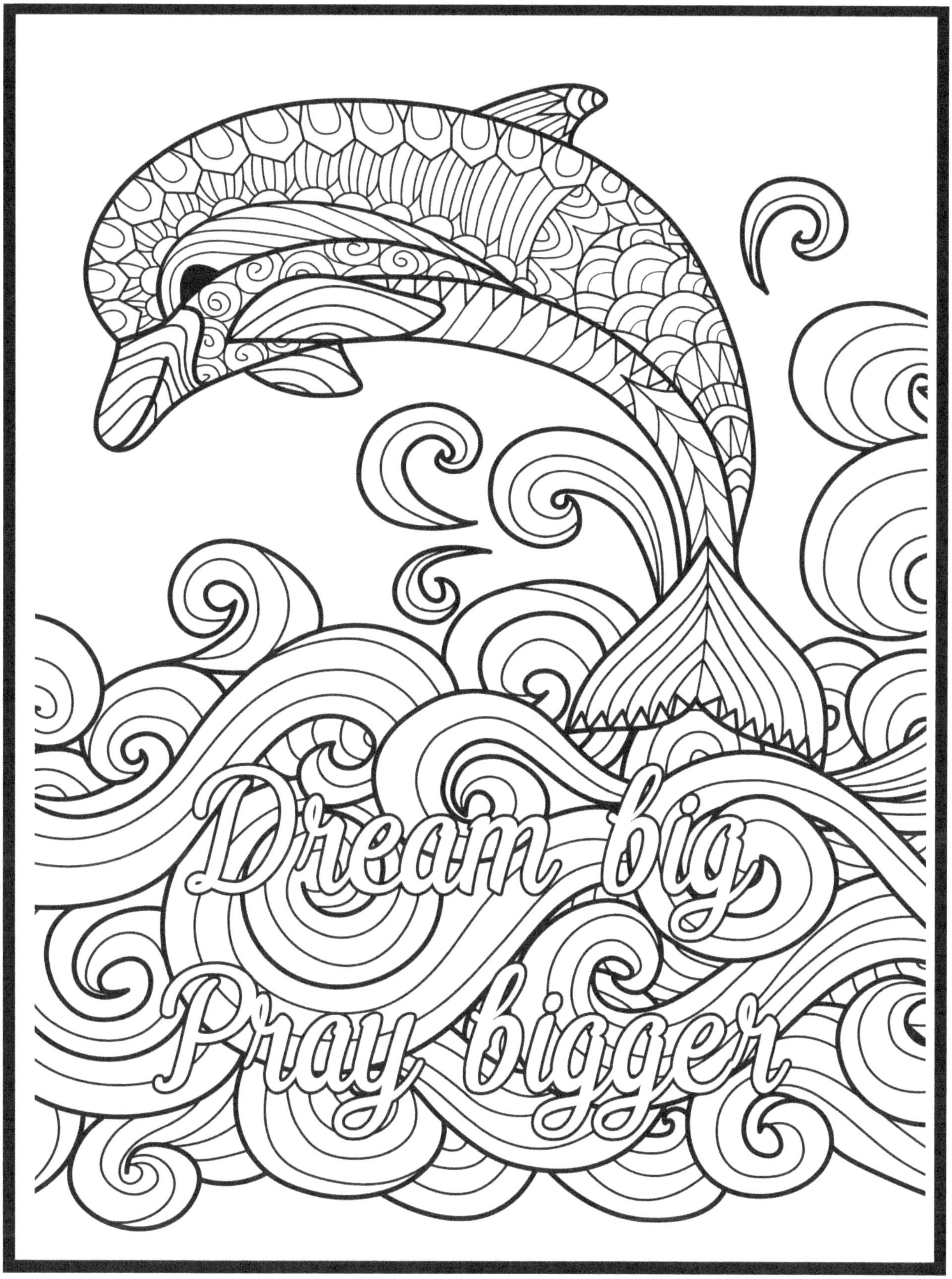
Dream big
Pray bigger

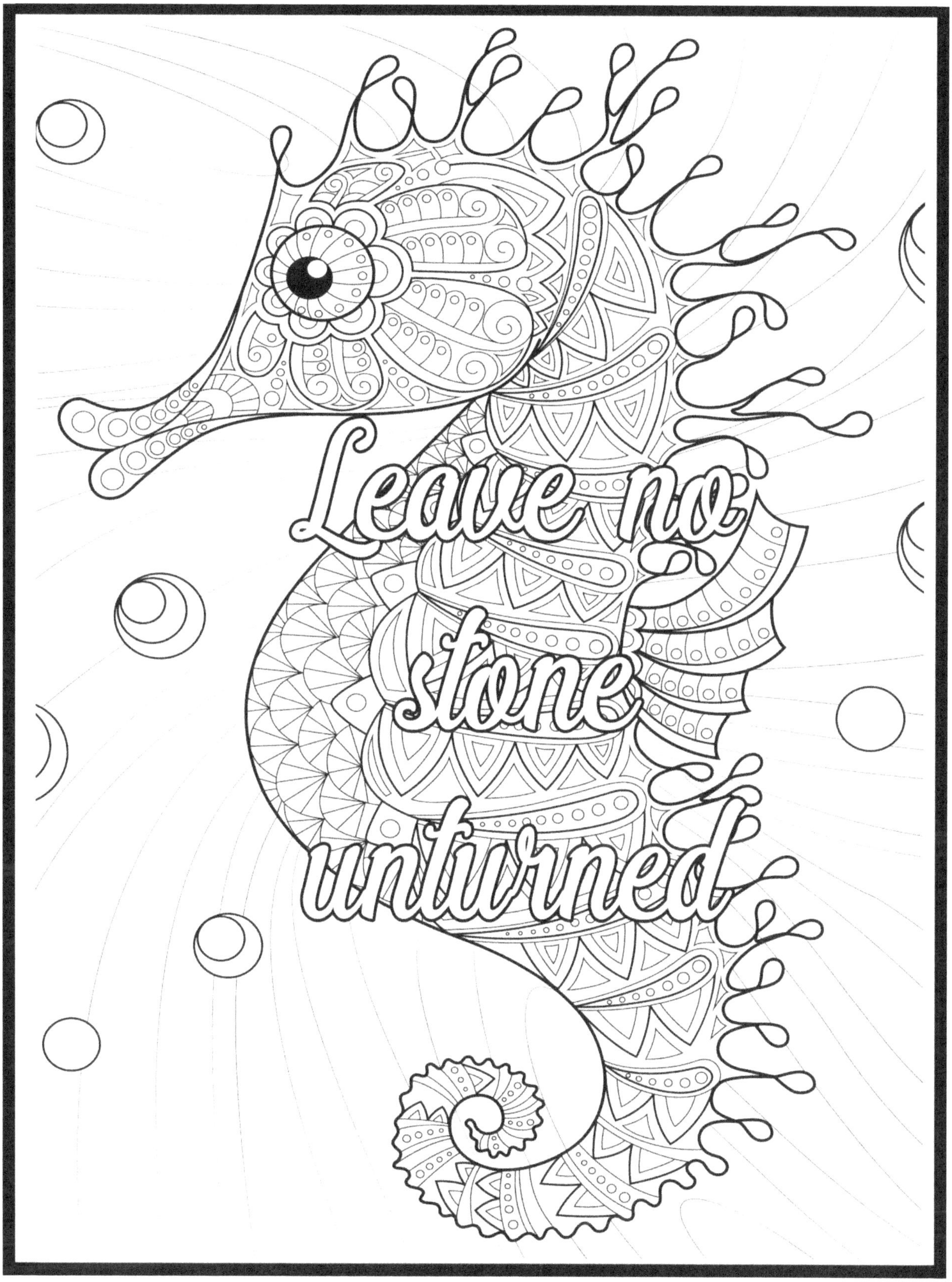
Leave no
stone
unturned

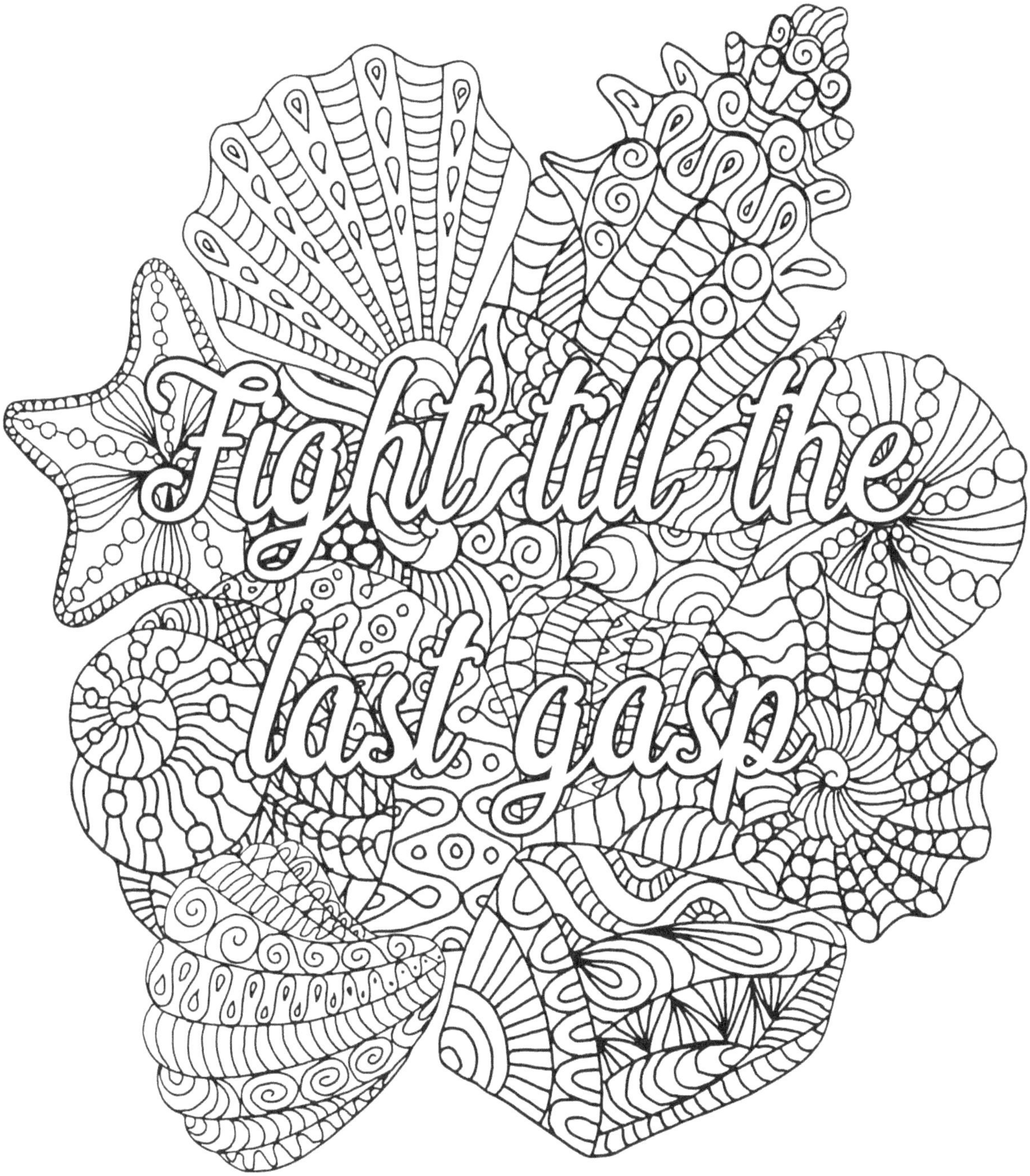
Fight till the
last gasp

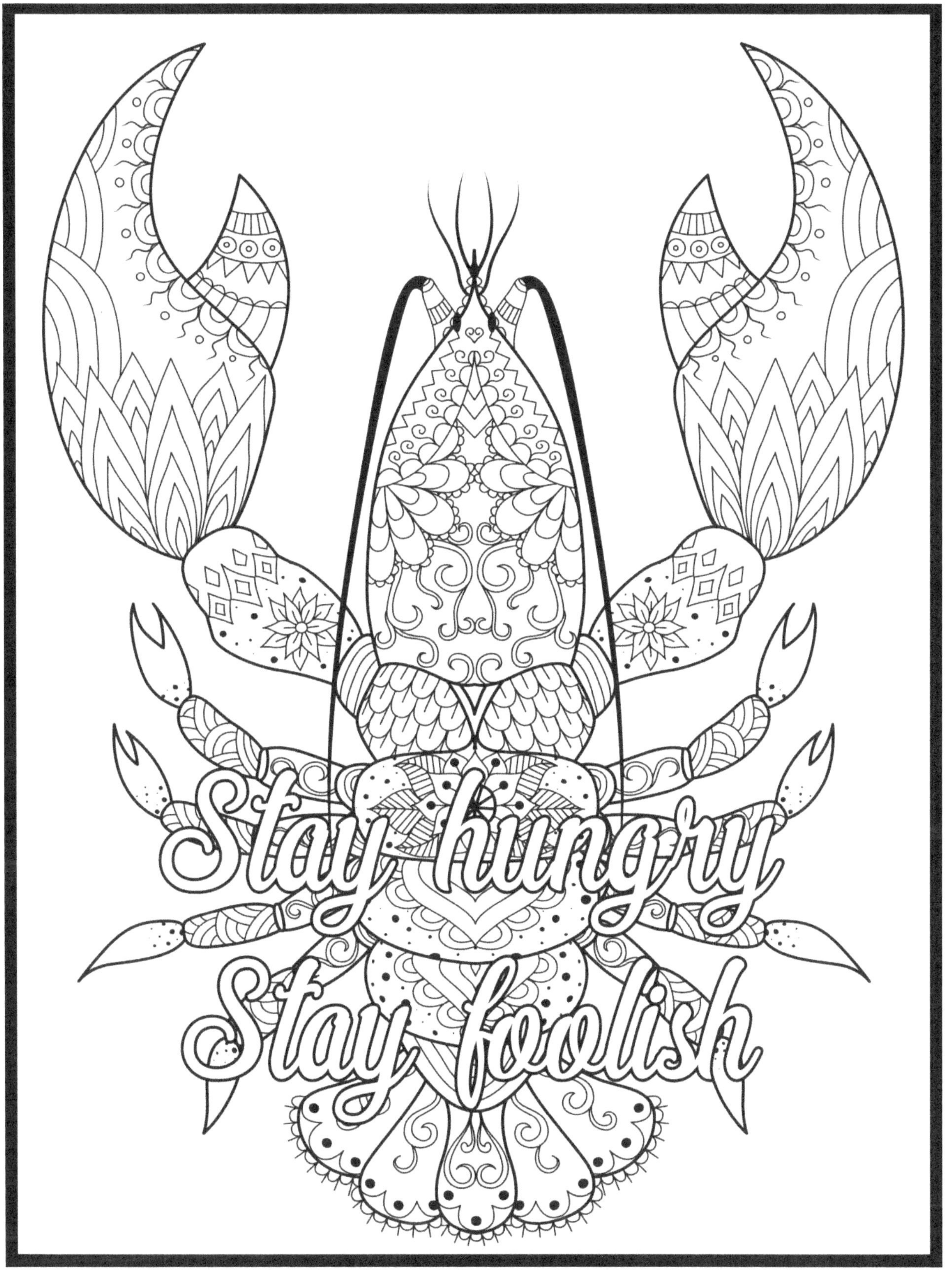
Stay hungry
Stay foolish

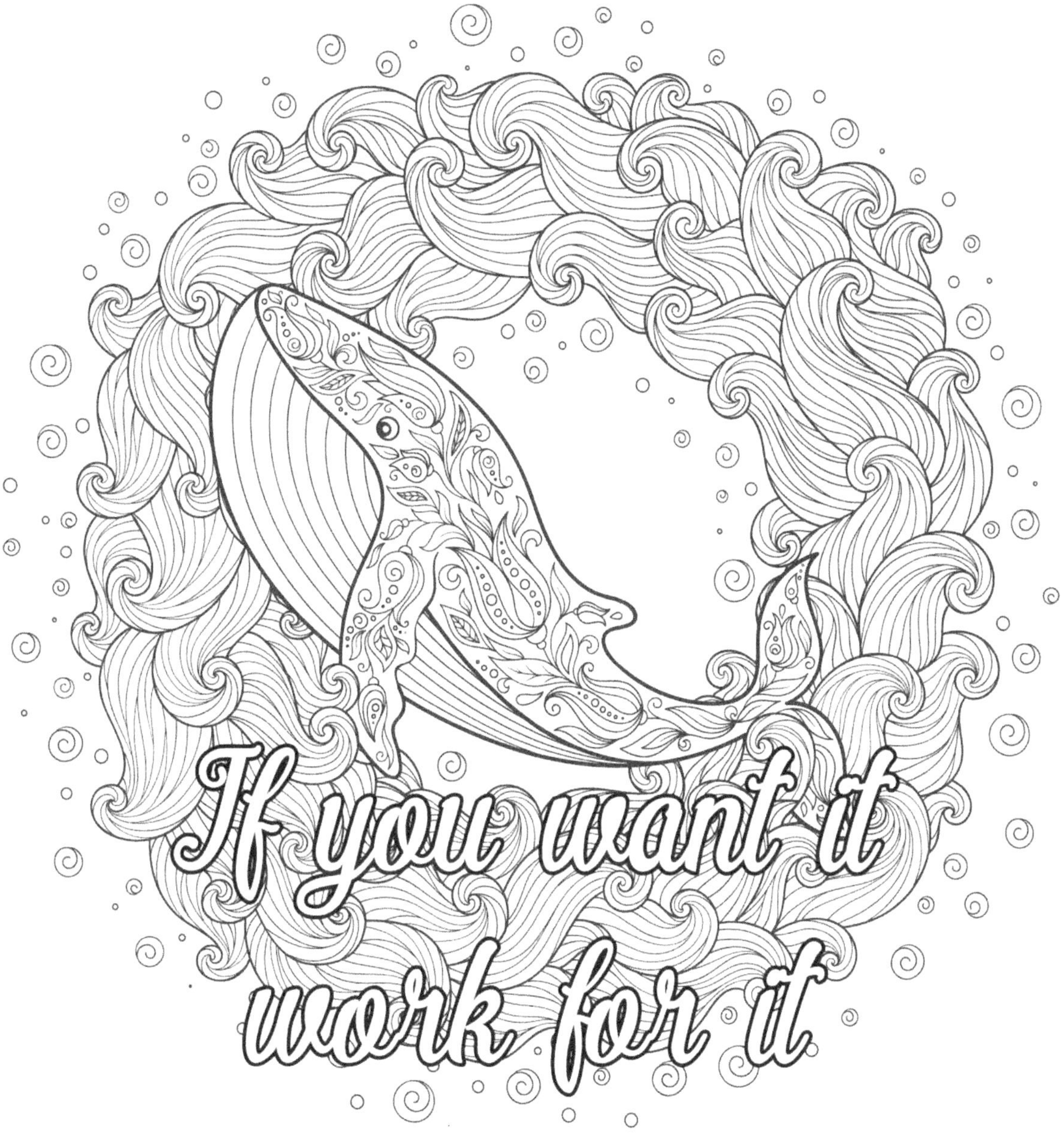
If you want it
work for it

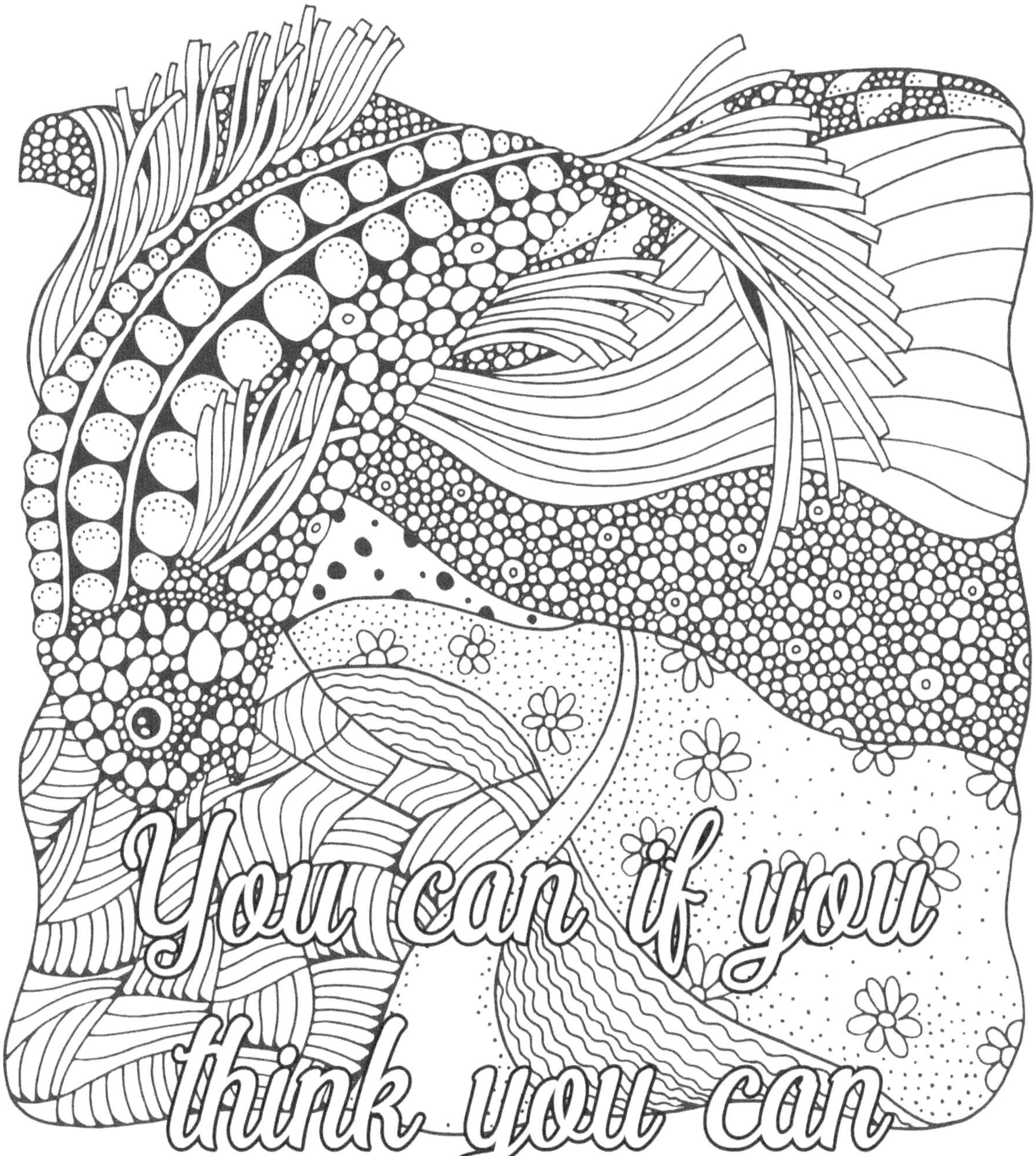
You can if you
think you can

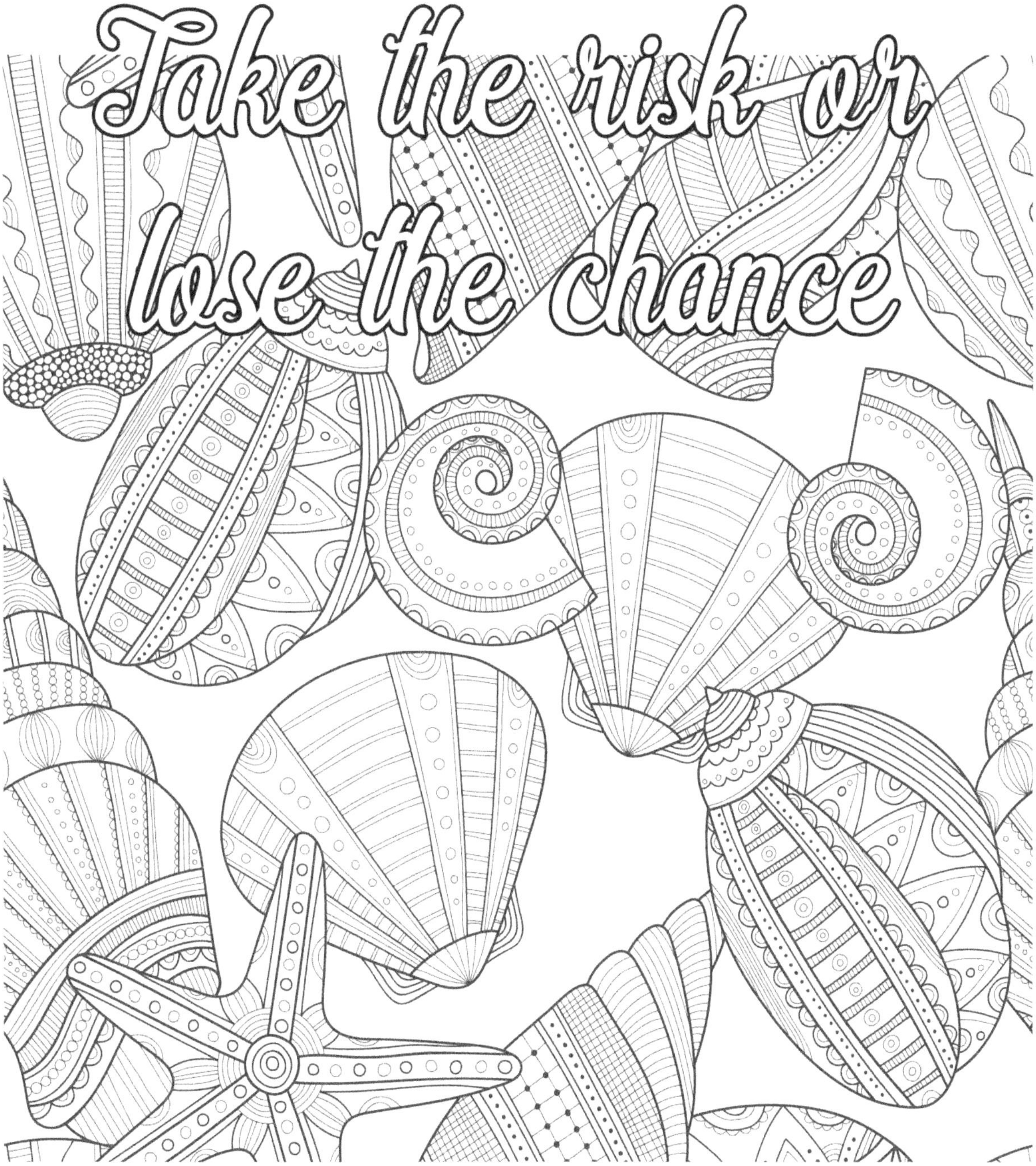
Take the risk or
lose the chance

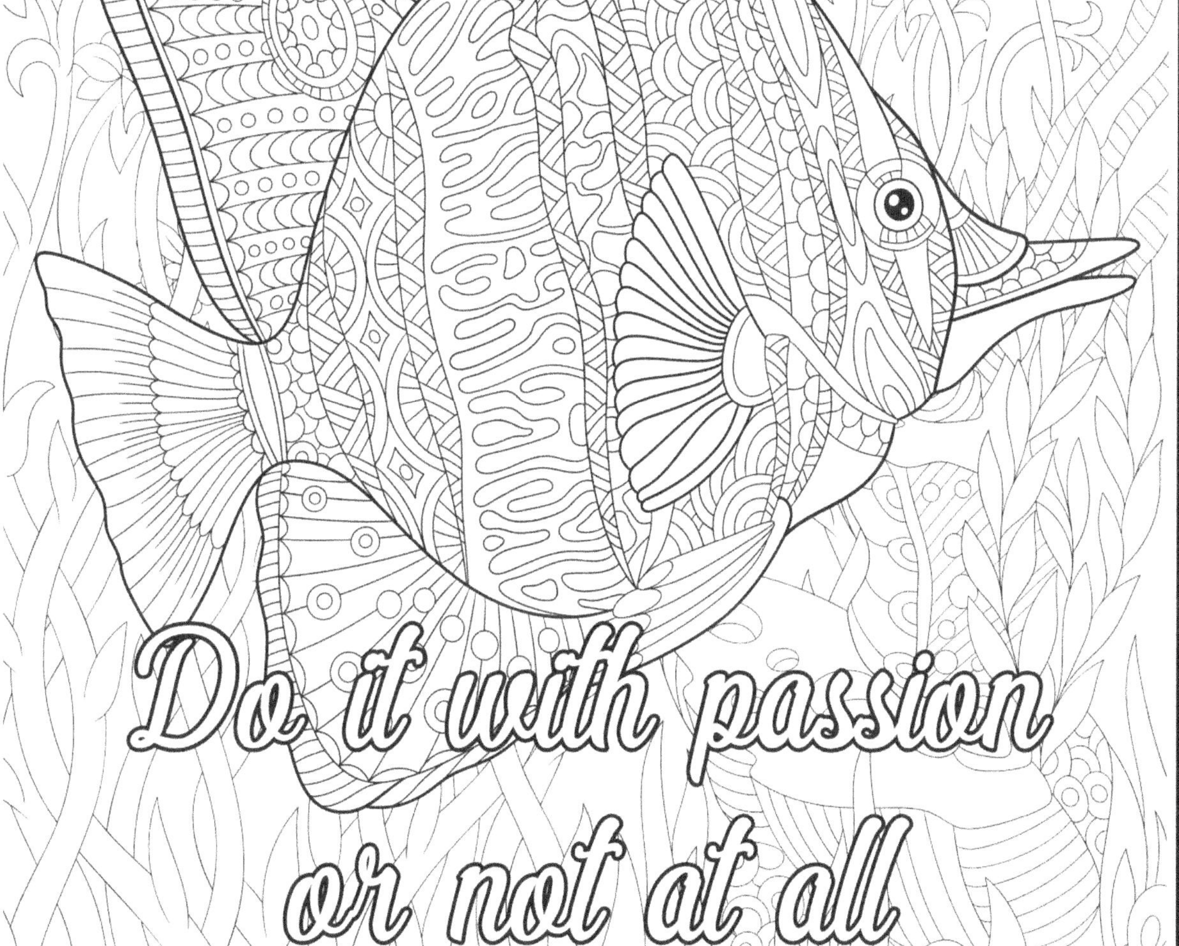
Do it with passion
or not at all

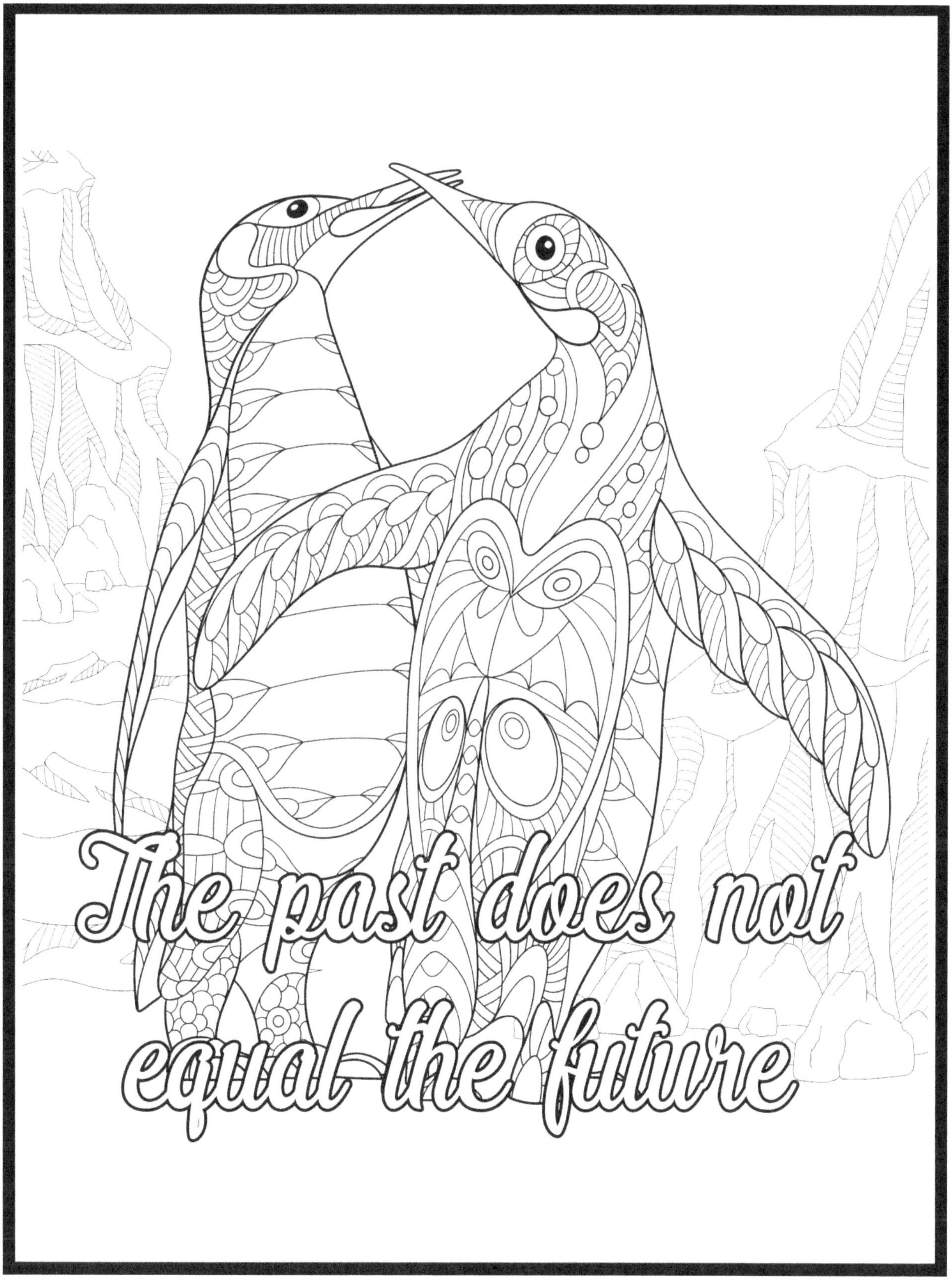
The past does not
equal the future

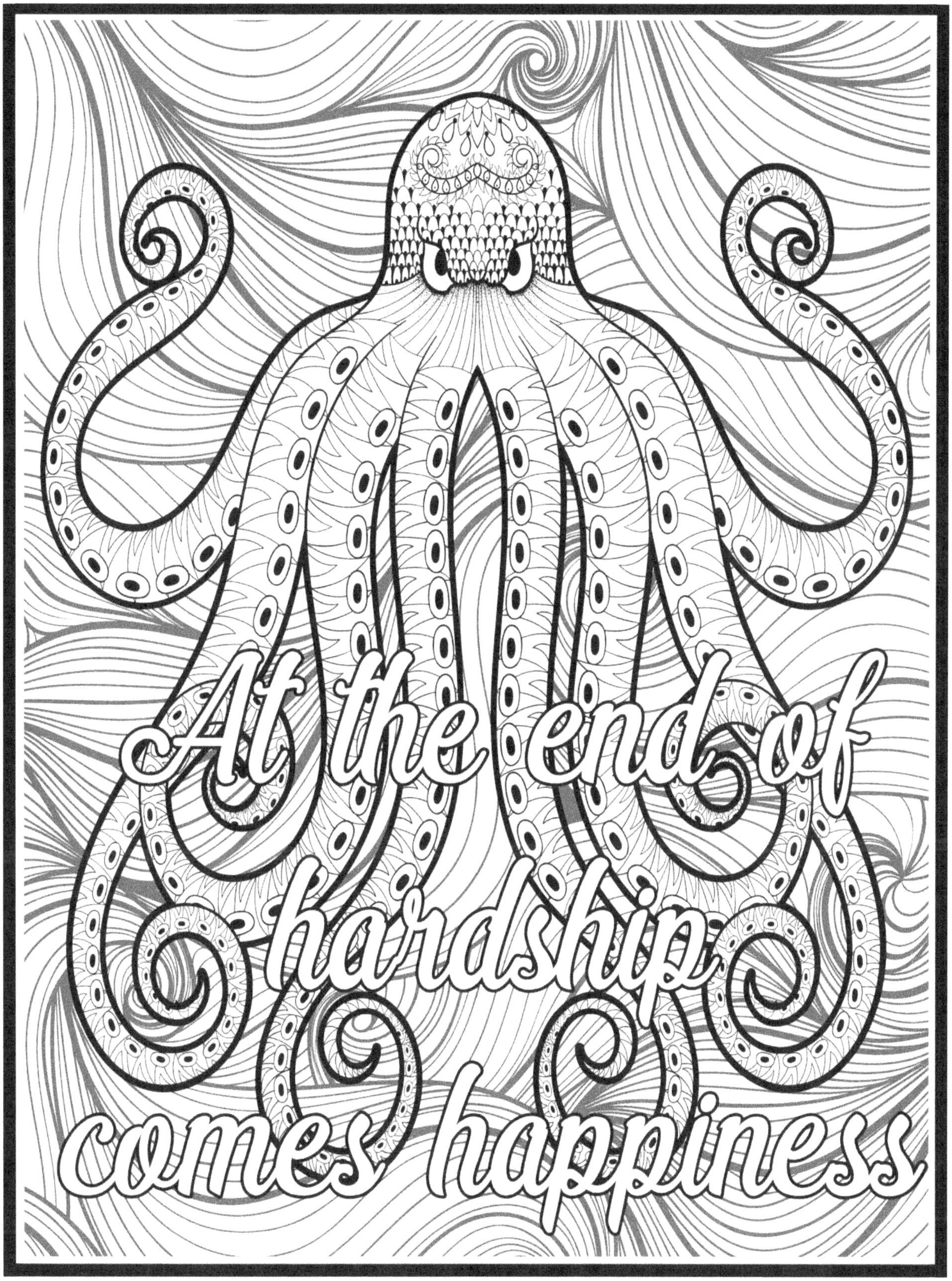
At the end of
hardship
comes happiness

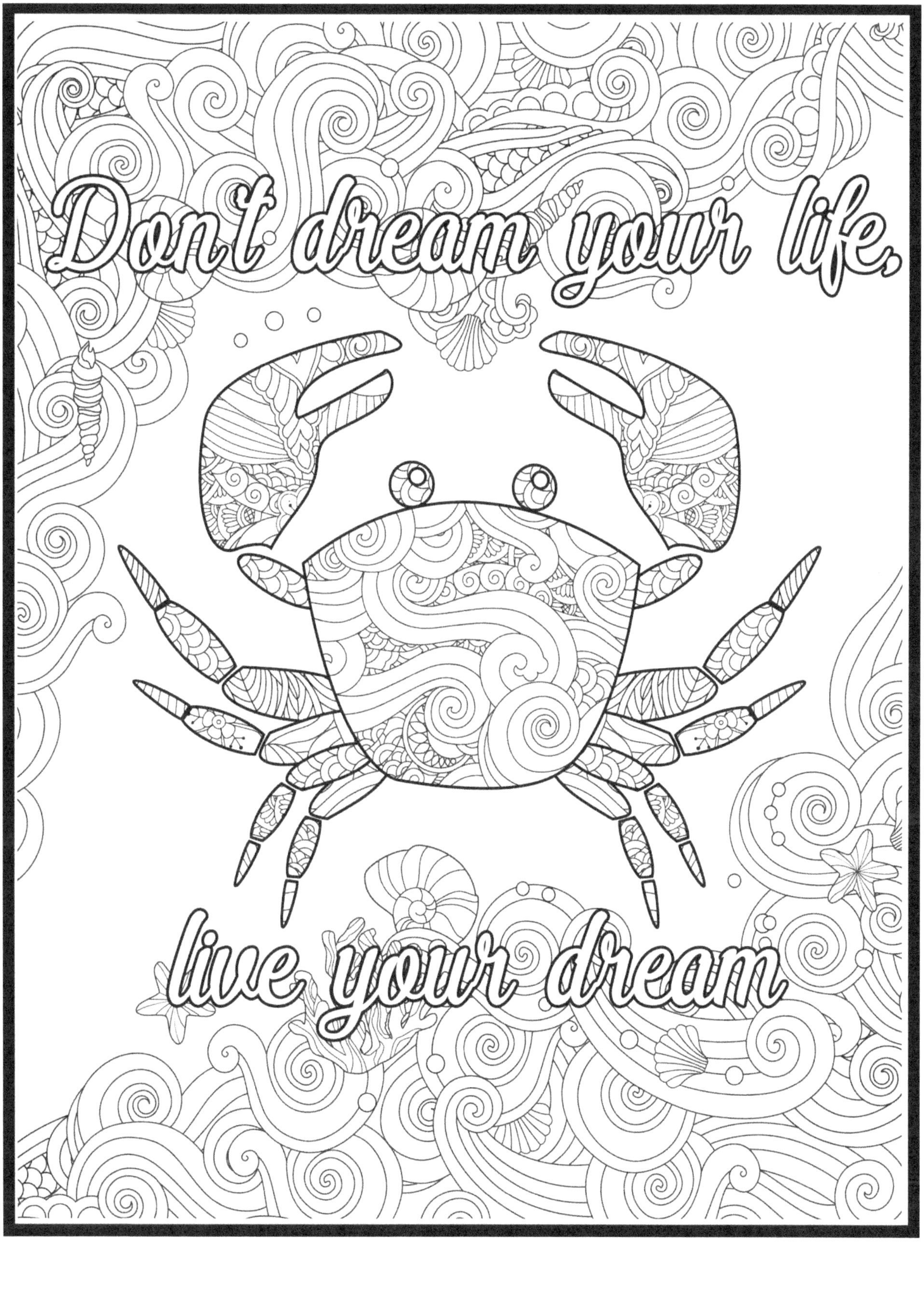
Don't dream your life,
live your dream

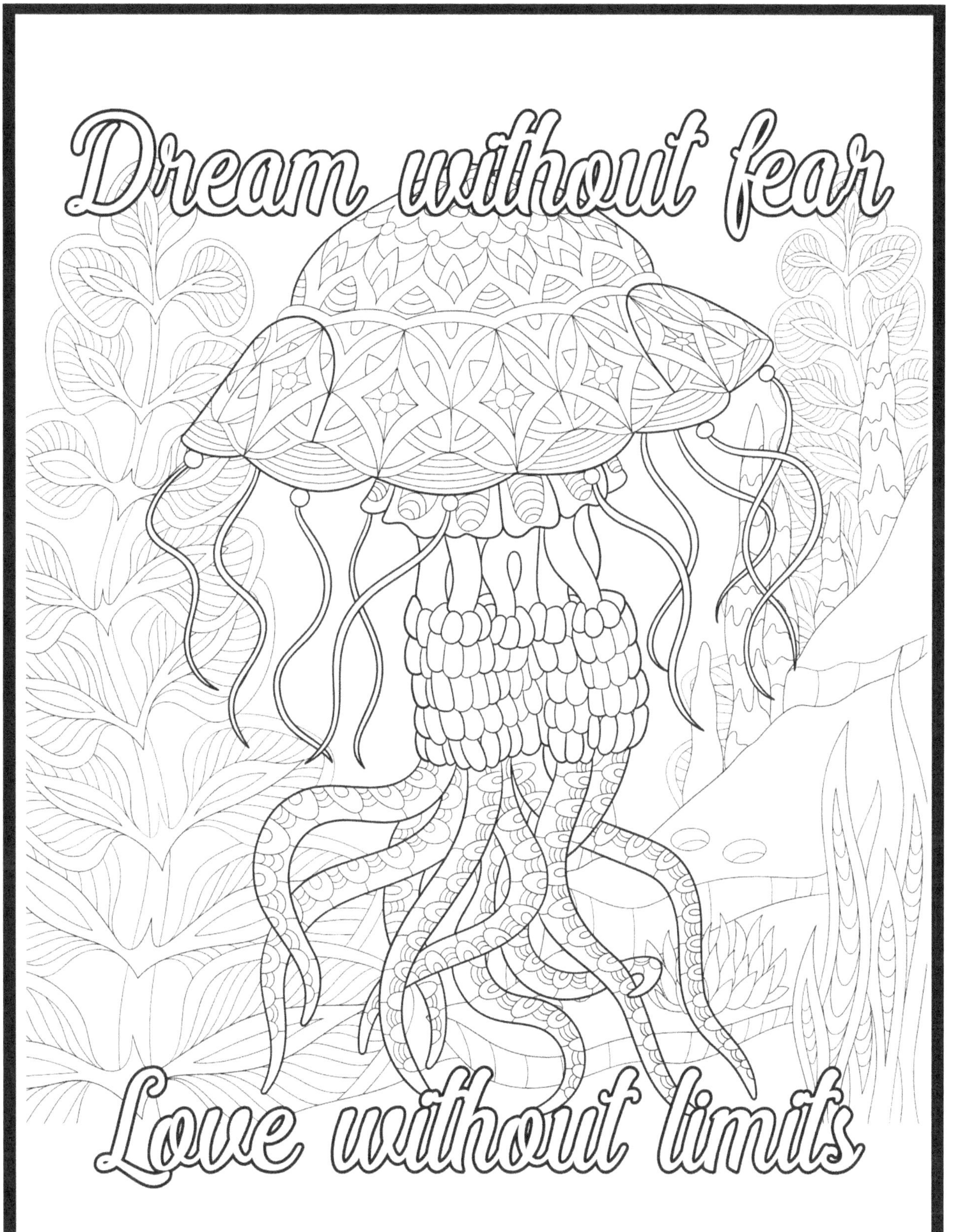
Dream without fear
Love without limits

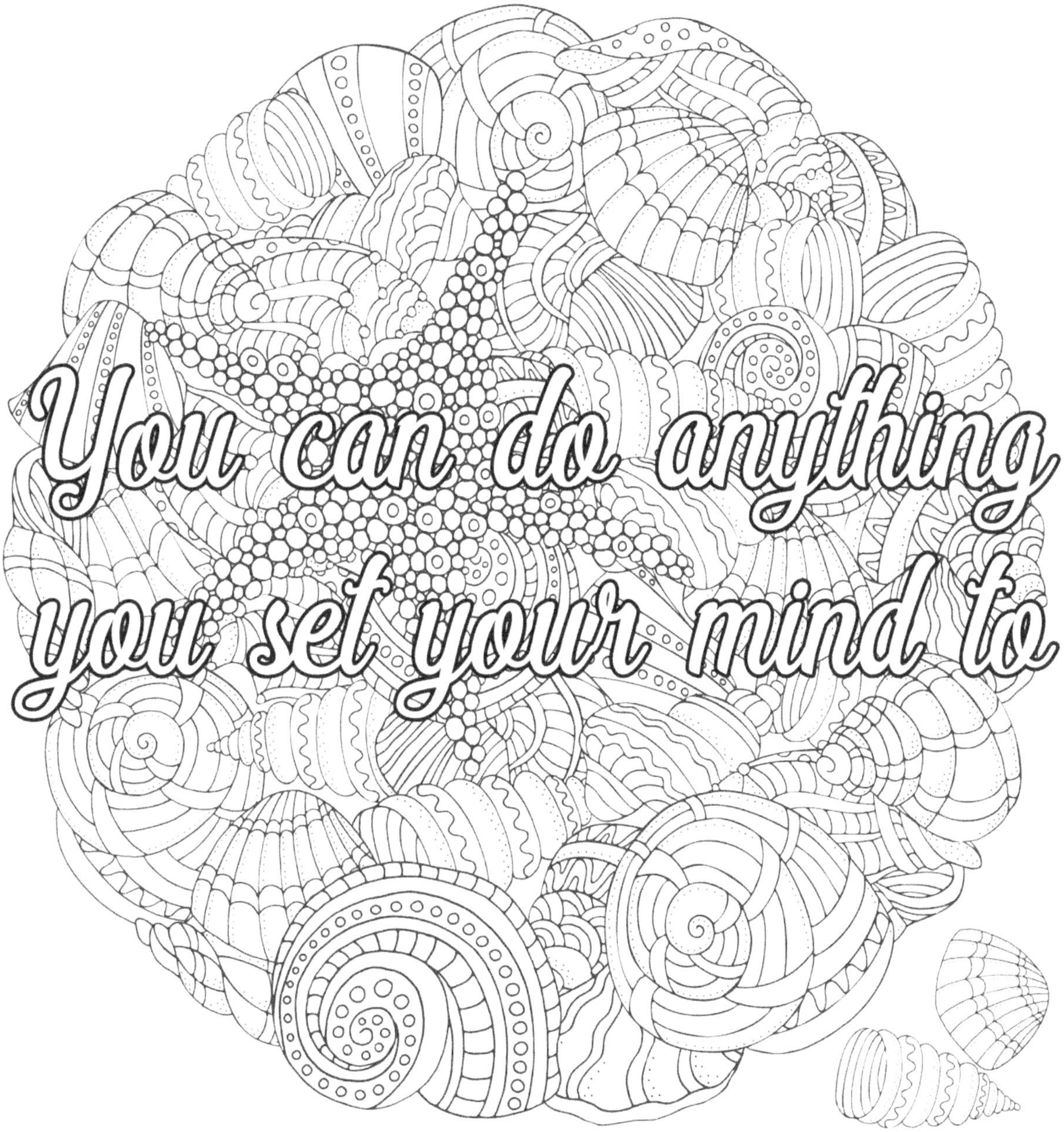
You can do anything
you set your mind to

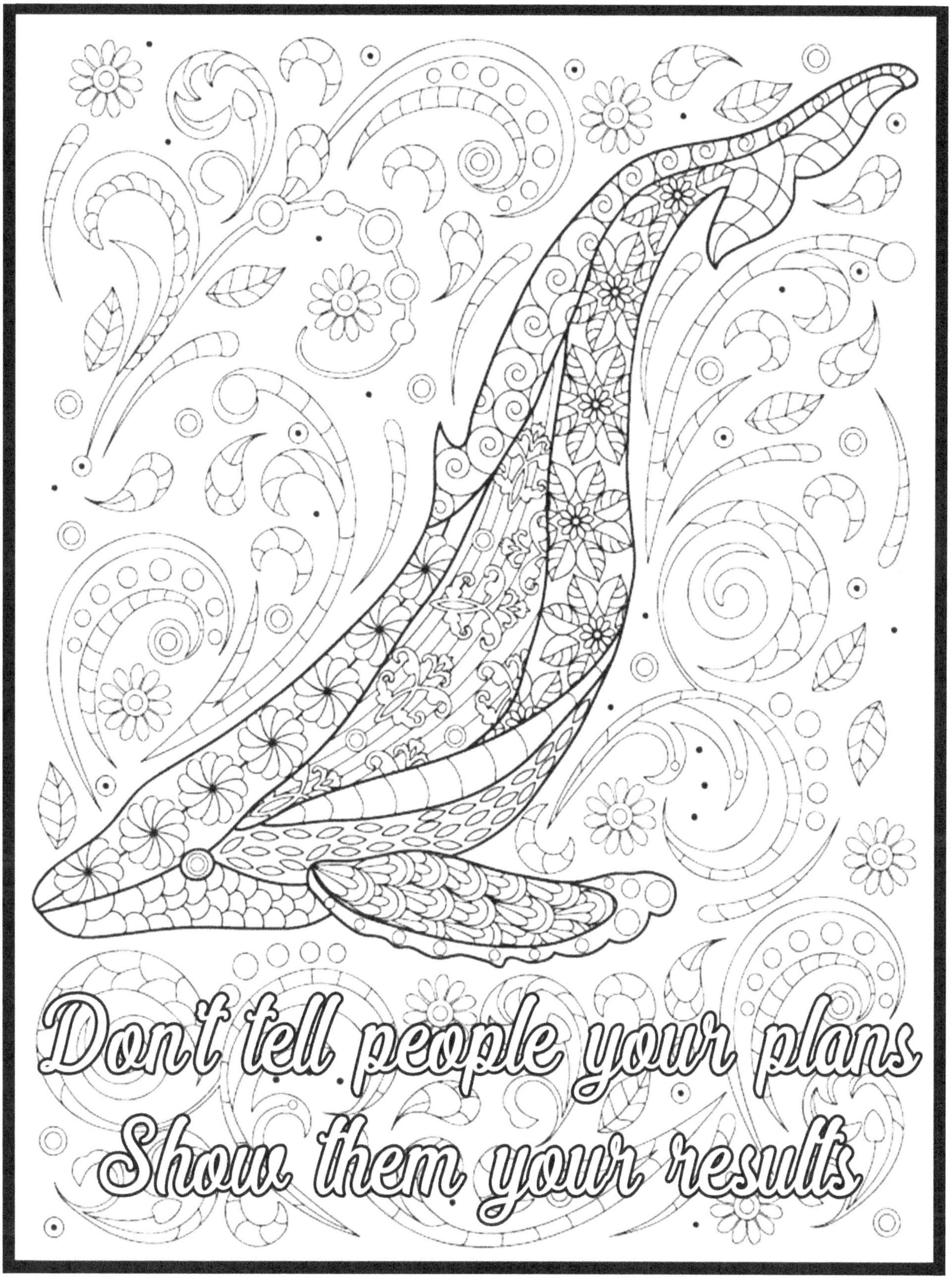
Don't tell people your plans
Show them your results

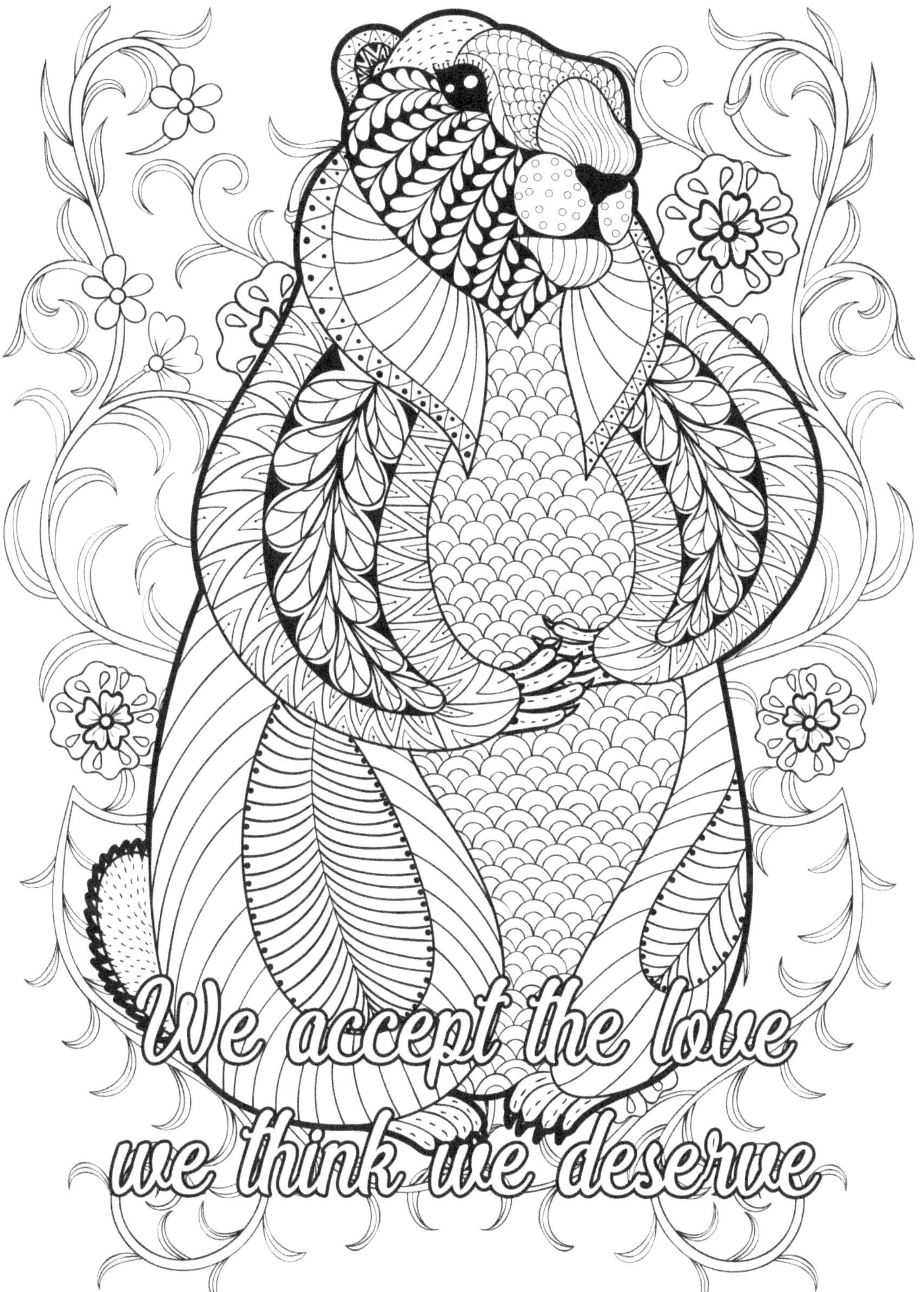
We accept the love
we think we deserve

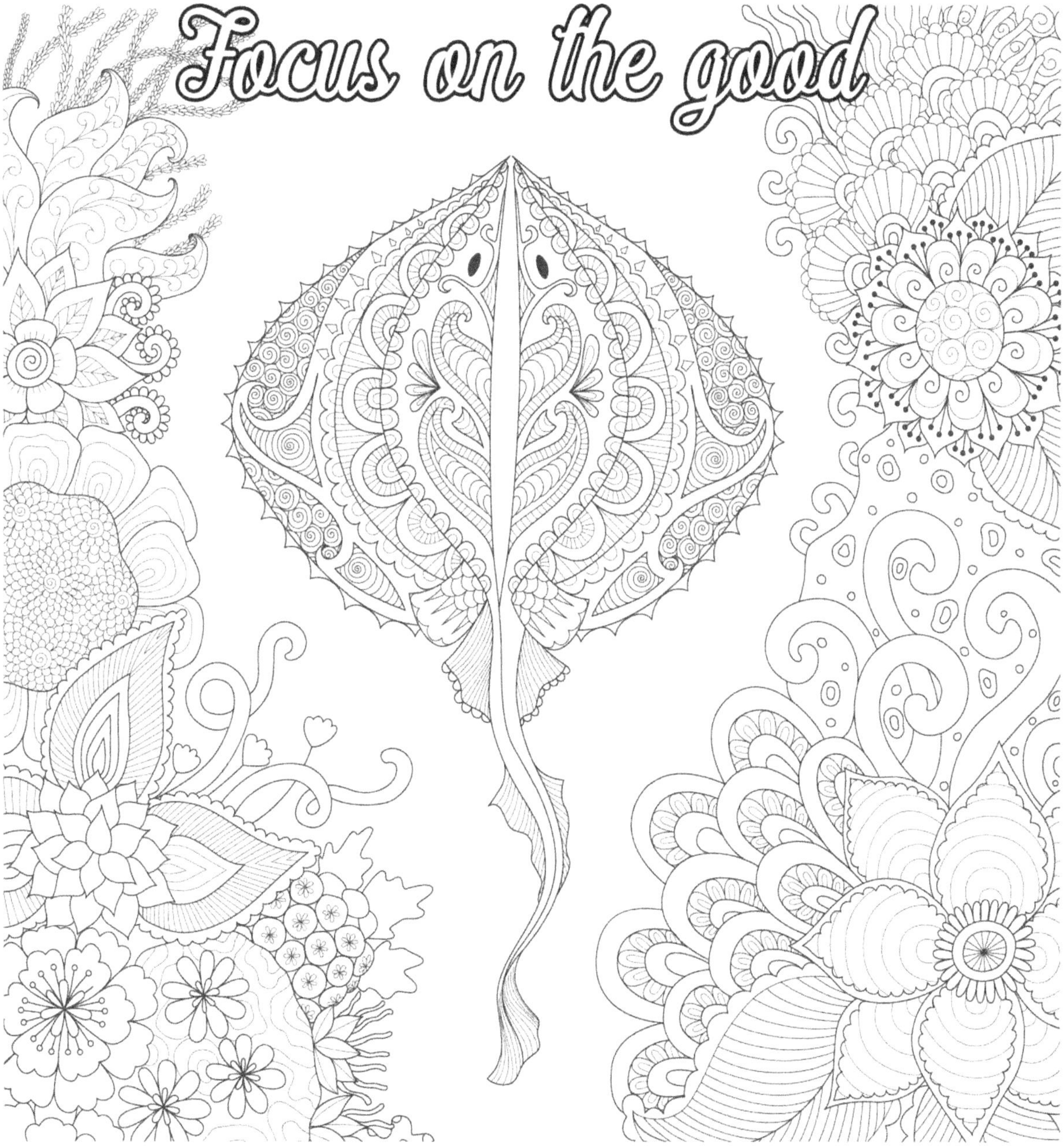
Focus on the good

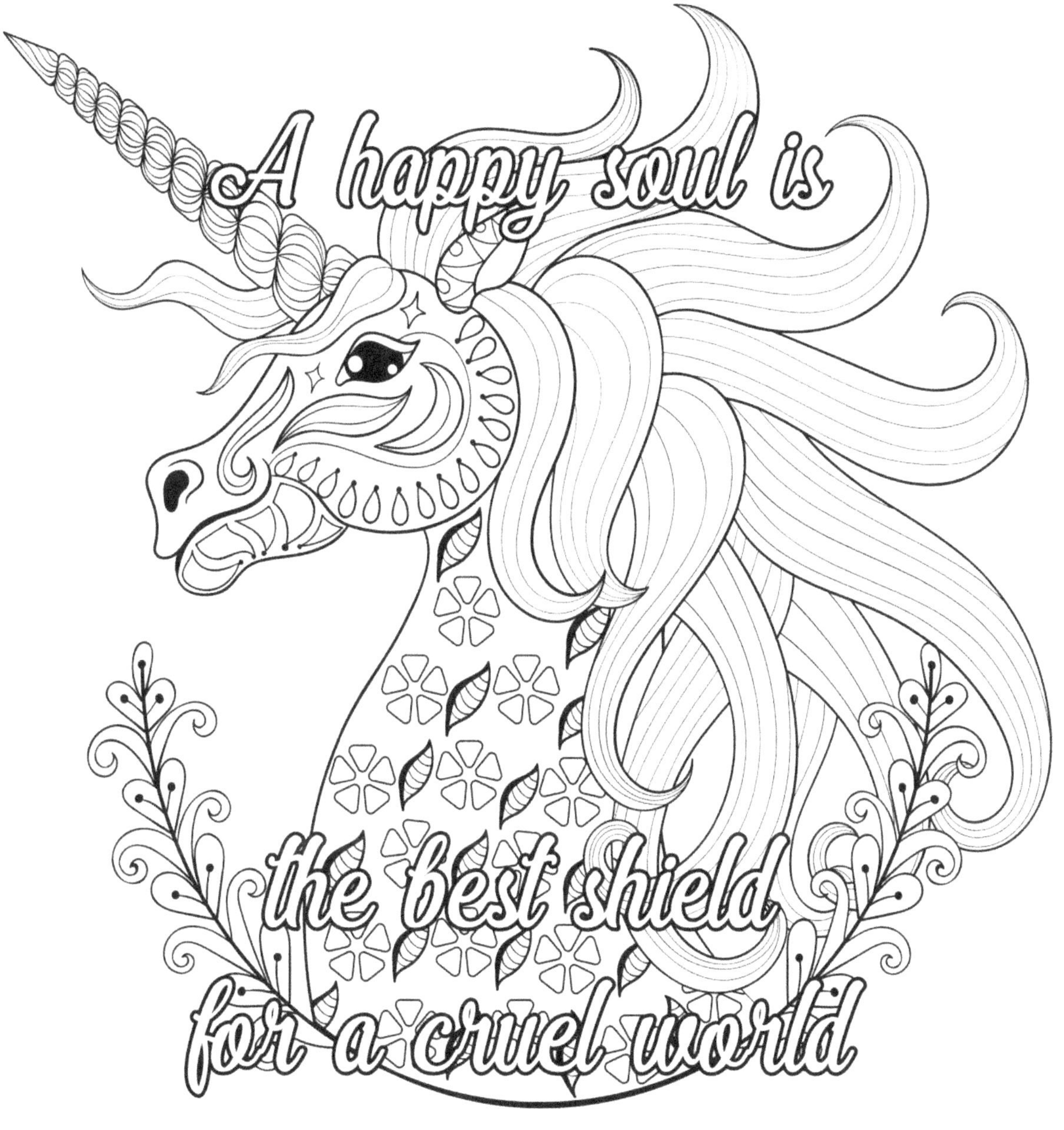
A happy soul is
the best shield
for a cruel world